THE
SHIPPING
FORECAST

CELEBRATING
100 YEARS

MEG CLOTHIER

BBC
BOOKS

BBC Books, an imprint of Ebury Publishing
Penguin Random House UK
One Embassy Gardens, 8 Viaduct Gardens,
Nine Elms, London SW11 7BW

BBC Books is part of the Penguin Random House group of companies whose addresses
can be found at global.penguinrandomhouse.com

Penguin
Random House
UK

First published by BBC Books in 2024

www.penguin.co.uk

A CIP catalogue record for this book is available from the British Library

ISBN 9781785949265

Images © Tabitha Mary Ltd. (p. x), Met Office (p. 12)
and Alamy (pp. 27, 90, 109, 135 and 150)

'Glanmore Sonnets VII' by Seamus Heaney from *New and Selected Poems 1966–1987*
is reprinted in this book by kind permission of Faber & Faber
'The Shipping Forecast' by John O'Donnell from *Sunlight: New and Selected Poems*
is reprinted in this book by kind permission of Dedalus Press
'Prayer' by Carol Ann Duffy from *Mean Time* (published by Pan Macmillan)
is reprinted in this book by kind permission of the poet

Printed and bound in Great Britain by Clays Ltd, Elcograf S.p.A.

The authorised representative in the EEA is Penguin Random House Ireland, Morrison
Chambers, 32 Nassau Street, Dublin D02 YH68.

Penguin Random House is committed to a sustainable future for our business, our readers
and our planet. This book is made from Forest Stewardship Council® certified paper.

MIX
Paper | Supporting
responsible forestry
FSC
www.fsc.org   FSC® C018179

For my brother

Enter Mariners, wet

The Tempest

CONTENTS

WELCOME ABOARD 1

WEATHER 3
WARNINGS 17
MAPS 39
CROSSINGS 57
TIDELINE 79
BOOTY 97
SOLO 117
STORY 139
OTHERWORLD 161
POETRY 181

REFERENCES 199
ACKNOWLEDGEMENTS 211
ABOUT THE AUTHOR 214

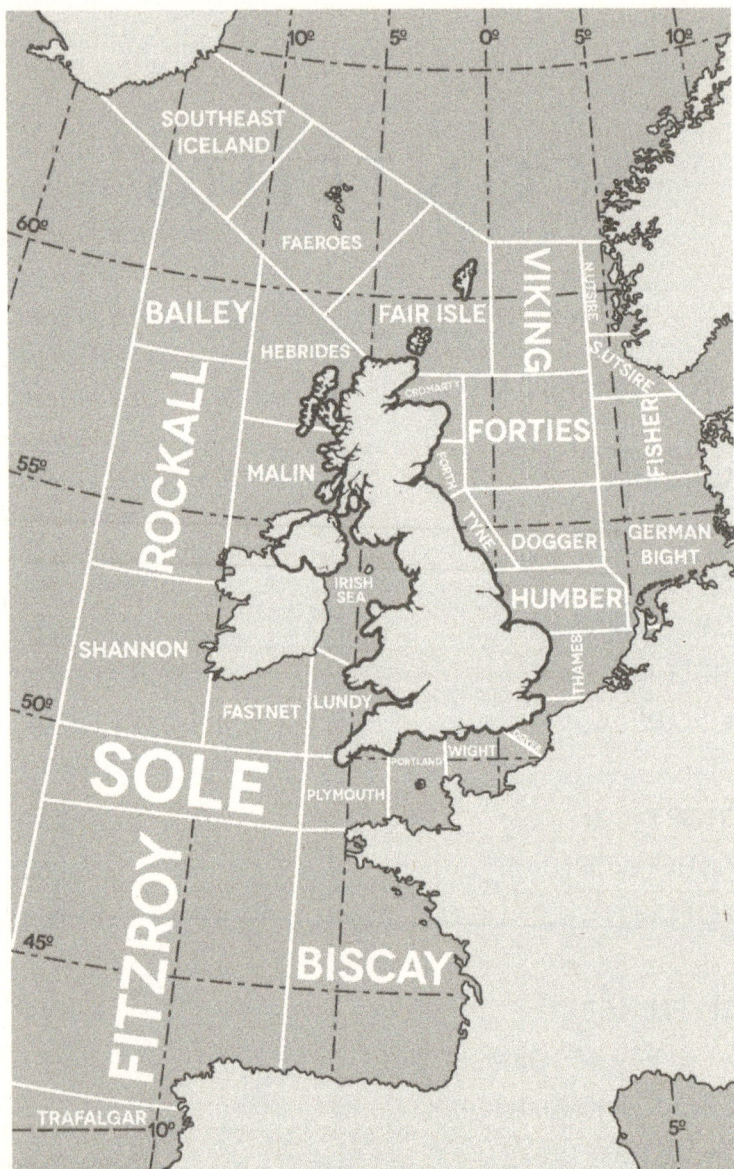

WELCOME
ABOARD

The *Shipping Forecast* is beautiful and useful. It's saved lives; it sparks joy. It's unapologetically geeky, but always stylish and slick. It whispers to us of adventure, of a life less ordinary, while being every bit as comforting as tea and toast. It's serious, yes, self-important, never – mock it, plunder it, remix it, whatever you do, you can't undermine it. It's subtly different every day, and yet it's unchanging and unchanged. And it's been equally important to the hoariest fisherman, the hardiest sailor and to the new mother who catches 'Sailing By' during the long watches of the night.

Frankly, there's never a bad time to hymn the *Shipping Forecast*'s myriad qualities, but the hundred-year anniversary is a golden opportunity to shout about that rare beast – a universally beloved British institution. It has weathered the choppy seas of the last hundred years to sail blithely into the twenty-first century, determinedly itself, as popular as ever.

The *Shipping Forecast*, I'd go so far as to say, encapsulates some of the best things about Britain: our passion for public service, our sense of adventure, our love of quirkiness, our offbeat creativity. But even more than that, in a few hundred words, this singular radio programme is a slipway to understanding a surprising amount of our history and our culture, our literature and our lore. With the *Shipping Forecast* as our compass, we can explore both our country and ourselves: the good, the bad – the wondrous and the weird.

Batten down the hatches. We're about to weigh anchor.

WEATHER

About to listen to SF + have a think

Note in an old logbook, 15 August 1999

47° 48' 40" N / 07° 24' 16" W

IF YOU, LIKE MANY PEOPLE, love the *Shipping Forecast* for reasons which have absolutely nothing to do with the meteorology, please skip instantly to WARNINGS. You might even consider skipping MAPS to OTHERWORLD as well, and starting at the end, which is all about the *poetry*. You could then work backwards, until you're braced for this chapter, which is, I warn you, going to be a slosh of cold hard scientific seawater right down the back of your neck. I'm going to take the magical, mystical words of the *Shipping Forecast* and suck all the magic, all the mystery, right back out of them.

Nowadays, nobody pretends that those who go down to the sea in ships, whether to do business or to marvel at the wonders of the deep, nobody pretends those container-ship captains and super-yacht skippers rely on the *Shipping Forecast* to save them from the stormy winds. Inshore, there's your mobile phone, the Met Office website.

There's coastguard briefings over VHF radio. Offshore, there's any number of fiendishly complex systems which will pipe info to your onboard computer via satellite or SSB radio. Nobody, I promise you, wants to read a book about *them*.

Instead, think of the *Shipping Forecast* as a Moana-style Polynesian canoe: main hull + balancing outrigger. A hundred years ago, the seafarers rode the main hull, with a few fascinated landlubbers on the outrigger. That's flipped. Nowadays, the lubbers have taken up the paddles, while the sea-dogs are along for the ride. And that's because, as a nation, we've taken the *Shipping Forecast* to our hearts.

When I first drafted this upwind flog of a chapter, I wrote, 'The *Shipping Forecast*, as everyone knows, is broadcast on Radio 4 four times a day.' I noted the times: 0048, 0520, 1201, 1754. I acknowledged that of the four, only dawn and middle-night go out on regular FM, with lunchtime and teatime relegated to long wave (along with God all year round and cricket in season). But time, it turned out, had overhauled me. Those long retro waves, so adept at reaching ships offshore, are sailing over the western horizon, bound for the Blessed Isles, there to dwell with mix-tapes and curdled-cream rotary phones. Today, we enjoy two forecasts a day during the working week, with a 1754 treat at the weekend.

The final four-bulletin day was Easter Sunday 2024. Weather-wise it had, by and large, turned out nice after one of the wettest winters since records began, but the forecast told us not to be complacent. There were warnings of gales in western areas, thanks to a low beetling from PLYMOUTH to FASTNET. A new low was lurking in DOGGER. Low one wasn't going to trouble us where we were holidaying near Whitby, but low two meant we spent Easter Monday eating scones while the rain lashed the windows of a tea-room. But it was the bulletin's grand finale, the area forecast for SOUTHEAST ICELAND, that was a real zinger: northeasterly 7 to severe gale 9, occasionally storm 10 at first – plus snow, poor visibility and *icing*. Icing, trust me, is *Shipping Forecast* nerd gold.

And so, without further ado, let's start decoding.

First, those gale warnings. These come at the top of the broadcast, pinpointing any of the 31 succulently named forecast areas where the wind is expected to blow force 8 or more in the next 24 hours. Your basic starter-gale isn't *necessarily* going to trouble a medium-to-large yacht, nor a biggish fishing boat, nor a ferry, tanker or container ship – so long as they have good visibility, good navigation equipment, enough sea room and no engine trouble. It would, however, be a total nightmare for a smaller boat.

Gales also turn shallower, inshore waters very ugly, very quickly: large seas build, making ports hard to enter and estuary bars impossible to cross. Plus, since the wind direction shifts dramatically when a gale passes, secure anchorages can become suddenly and frighteningly untenable. In other words, possibly counter-intuitively, if you're out at sea when a gale hits, you're often better off as far away from land as possible.

If you ratchet another step up the Beaufort scale, you'll find that, with the same caveats, force 9 is just about survivable. Storm 10, on the other hand, which is like sticking your head out of a car window that's doing 60 miles per hour, feels like the foothills of Armageddon. Thankfully, I've never experienced 11 or 12, but I imagine the less said about them, the better.

Next comes the general synopsis. A normal radio or television weather synopsis radiates bonhomie. The affable presenter agrees the weather has been dreadful, and either promises relief or apologises that there's worse yet to come. The *Shipping Forecast* synopsis, by contrast, is a cool, calm and collected account of where stand the peaks of high pressure and the troughs of low pressure in our corner of the Atlantic. It's this celestial view, this lofty contour map, which allows us to predict the wind, the rain, the weather.

High-pressure weather, whether in summer or winter, is *nice* weather. It is the twinkly smile of Father Christmas. It is the dew on the Easter Bunny's paws. It is pink wine and barbecues and a *proper* bonfire night. But high-pressure weather, alas, is the exception rather than the rule. Why? Because the various islands we call home rise from the sea slap-bang in the path of an endless cavalcade of low-pressure systems, which clatter towards us across the Atlantic, like bowling balls hurled by the weather gods. Sometimes, those balls fall into the gutters to the north or south of us, but more often than not they strike.

It's a different story further south, closer to the equator. There the trade winds blow from the northeast, so equably, steadily and predictably that three weeks at sea crossing the Atlantic east–west is a breeze compared with just 24 short hours in the Western Approaches to the English Channel. Mariner-turned-writer Joseph Conrad, in his sort-of-autobiography *The Mirror of the Sea*, tells us the trade winds are like monarchs of long-established kingdoms, where stable institutions check undue ambition. But here in Britain, says Conrad, we're governed by a more despotic ruler. 'Clothed in a mantle of dazzling gold or draped in rags of black clouds like a beggar, the might of the Westerly Wind sits enthroned upon the western horizon with the whole North Atlantic as a footstool for his feet and the first twinkling stars making a diadem for his brow.'*

The general synopsis, therefore, helps us understand what sort of mood the West Wind is in, what he's got up his sleeve – how big, you might say, his balls are. A deep low to the west, moving fast to the east, is a hairy scary ball. A shallow low to the east, a low that is, to coin a phrase, *losing its identity*, is not a ball over which you need lose any sleep. Why does it matter whether the lows are deep or shallow? Because air moves from high pressure to low pressure, so the bigger the pressure difference, the steeper the slope, the faster the balls, the bigger the wind, the bigger the waves. Those, pretty much, are the rules of the game.

And now for the area forecasts, a giant hopscotch grid chalked for the West Wind and his minions. We start at VIKING, off the coast of Norway obvs, and march south through the North Sea, taking in a GERMAN BIGHT, before turning west along the north coast of France, braving BISCAY and bottoming out at TRAFALGAR, not all that far from where the trade winds kick in. Next we turn, possibly reluctantly, back north, mop up the Bristol

---

* What the sea's mirror reveals does rather depend on who's doing the looking. In Conrad's case, it shows his deep-seated mistrust of democracy, hence his affection for aerial autocrats.

Channel and the IRISH SEA, leave the island of Ireland and the HEBRIDES to starboard, before finishing up in SOUTHEAST ICELAND.

For each area you hear:

1. Wind direction and speed, what you can expect in the next 24 hours. Variable and cyclonic function as get-out clauses for when the wind's all over the shop, either because there's none to speak of, or because a depression's barrelling through.
2. Weather, be that vanilla showers, squally showers, wintry showers, thundery showers, rain or snow. Or fair. To be fair, sometimes it is fair.
3. Visibility, that infamous falling cadence. Good. Moderate. Poor. Technically, it's about how far you can see, so many metres, so many nautical miles, and not a moral judgement delivered by some godling inside Broadcasting House, who's wondering why you're still up at 0048 on a school-night, shovelling down toast to mop up the five pints you drank in the pub after work. Very poor indeed.

What the *Shipping Forecast* doesn't tell you about, or at least not explicitly, are fronts, which are those pencil strokes, decorated with semi-circles, triangles, or a mixture of the

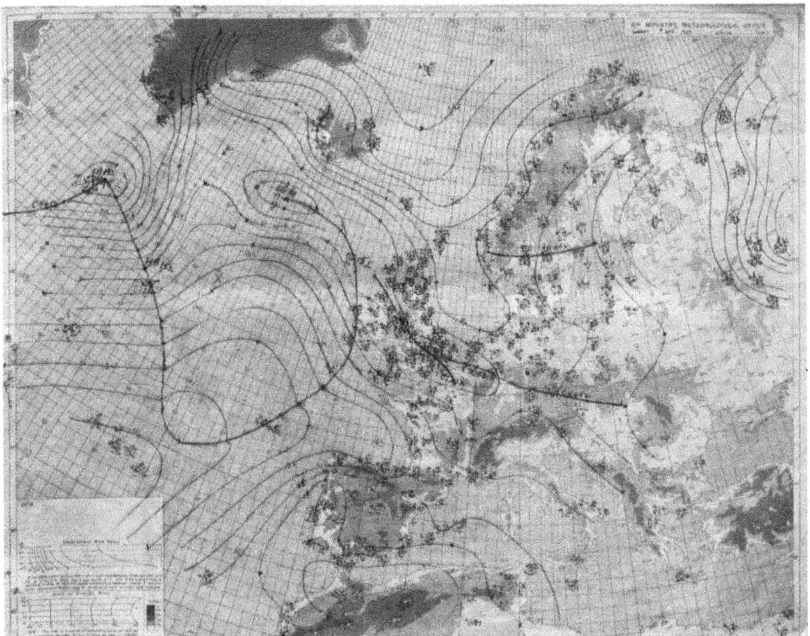
MINISTRY METEOROLOGICAL OFFICE

two, which dangle off areas of low pressure, like a spindly pair of legs.

While you're waiting for a depression to hit, you're looking at what Conrad calls the *southwesterly* face of the West Wind. The barometer is falling. The wind is building. You're tense. You're wondering if the gale will be as bad as the forecast says, or if in fact it'll be worse. The monarch's mood is 'brooding and veiled violence'. Then the warm front (semi-circles! like suns!) arrives. That might sound like a good thing, but it's actually the moment the rain hits and the wind really starts to blow. If you're out at sea, there's nothing for it but to endure hours of wet windy horrible weather – until the cold front (triangles! like icicles!) catches up. That might sound like a bad thing, but it's actually the moment the end is in sight. The wind shifts, ushering in the 'sparkling, flashing, cutting, clear-eyed anger' of the West Wind's *northwesterly* mood. There'll be squalls, showers, mad gusts, irruptions of hail, drama, denouement, resolution: slowly but surely the wind will start to drop.

The first gale I experienced at sea, crossing the Bay of Biscay in 1999 when I was 21, was a textbook introduction to how the warm front is a portentous opening number, and how the cold front is a rousing curtain call. It was, I admit, only a wannabe gale, the West Wind had only sent his dauphin, but it was the top of force 7, and it was gusting 8, and we were beating into it, and it was the first time my brother and I had skippered a boat alone, so at the time it felt like a storm for the ages. Here are the scribbled notes from our rumpled logbook.

0000–0400 promised SWs arrived. No more than 6 as yet. Staysail and 2 reefs great in gusts, underpowered in lulls. A cautious sail plan if ever I saw one. The barometer's dropping steadily ahead of the low but, according to Met Office definitions, it's falling, not falling fast.

0810 we just had a beast of a squall, 45 across deck. Bed for me. That'll be the warm front arriving. The entry's in my brother's handwriting, so I've just relieved him after he stood the 0400–0800 watch. I expect he's about to make me tea and toast.

1130 gusts getting bigger. Third reef in. This is us slugging it out between the two fronts. Every five minutes there'll be a *whump* as the bow buts a wave, a *kreeeeesh* as the spray sweeps the decks. Sort of fun and sort of not.

1845 Lot of rain. Crew praying this might be the Thing passing. This *is* the cold front passing.

2000 Spectacular rainbow. Wind veered to NW + dropped to 20 KTS. It's over!

Before we committed to the crossing, we had, of course, listened to the *Shipping Forecast*, heads bowed over paper and pencils, tummies still roiling after flogging round Portland Bill. If the voice had said, 'There are warnings of gales in BISCAY,' we'd have spun the wheel hard to starboard, and found safe harbour somewhere in PLYMOUTH long before it hit. As it was, the voice said 7, and we took a small gamble: we were young, fearless and we wanted to get to Spain. The small gamble paid off. We had the mini-adventure we'd signed up for.

But what if the forecast had been wrong? What if the wind had actually blown 8 – or 9 – or 10? What would have happened then? But we, of course, had faith in the *Shipping Forecast*. No revolution is going to turn the West Wind into a defanged constitutional monarch any time soon, but the meteorologists who have devoted their lives to studying his temper shield us from the worst of his wrath.

It used to be a very different story …

WARNINGS

I have a leech in a bottle, my dear,
that foretells all these prodigies
and convulsions of nature

The poet William Cowper in a letter to his cousin (1787)

THE FIRST *SHIPPING FORECAST* wasn't issued by the Met Office. It was issued by a god. We can't be sure whether it was water god Enki tipping off Utnapishtim, or fire god Prometheus tipping off Deucalion, or storm god Yahweh tipping off Noah, but we do know that humanity's towering thunderhead of solipsism means we've long thought bad weather was our fault. It was, literally, all about us. We were bad. A god would issue a storm warning. The lucky few would listen. The storms would come; the waters would rise. The unlucky many would drown. The survivors would try, really very hard, to do better next time.

In 1703, Britain was struck by what felt like (and perhaps was) the worst storm in our history. The lives of thousands of sailors and fishermen were lost at sea. A fifth of the naval fleet was wrecked. Hundreds of people drowned when a storm-surge flooded the Somerset Levels. Church spires crashed. Windmills crumbled. But despite its unprecedented ferocity, the people who lived through it, says Martin Brayne in his account *The Greatest Storm*, knew precisely what was going on: 'It was, quite literally, an Act of God: a blow deliberately delivered by an all-powerful, omniscient deity as a warning and in anger.' Today, we'd demand an inquiry. Back then, Queen Anne's government declared a national day of fasting.

We know all about the Great Storm thanks to Daniel Defoe, a jobbing journalist in his forties, not yet the fêted author of *Robinson Crusoe*. In an age of coffee-houses, news-sheets and gossip, he put out a call for first-hand reports, like a slo-mo, but no less effective, social media shout-out. Intelligence poured in from all over the country, and from it he crafted a book, a quick-and-dirty first draft of history. But before he gets into the particulars, his intro states that here was proof, if ever proof was needed, of the existence of a supreme being. 'I cannot doubt but the Atheist's hard'ned Soul trembl'd a little as well as his House, and he felt some Nature asking him some little Questions as these. Am not I mistaken? Certainly there is some such thing as a God.' Other men, Defoe allows, will nonetheless try to interrogate Nature, will try to understand how such a storm could have come to pass, but she (always *she* ...) will deny them, saying: 'It is not in Me, you must go Home and ask my Father.' It was, in theory, the Age of Enlightenment, but he seems rather pleased that the Almighty's wind has snuffed 'the Candle of Reason' right out.

One thing, though, was true: many, many people, and good Christians at that, were trying to get Nature to spill her beans. For a long time, embryonic meteorologists had leant hard on Aristotle, whose crackpot theories about everything from the sex life of eels to the inferiority of women were treated with extreme deference until really very recently. His *Meteorologica* (i.e. the study of things high up), in a nutshell, said different exhalations produce different phenomena. Hot dry exhalations: wind, meteors, thunder and lightning. Cold, wet exhalations: clouds, dew, rain. All gloriously wrong, of course, but Aristotle always sounds so sure of himself, it's hard not to believe him.

Then, before the Enlightenment really got going, back when astrology, alchemy and other pseudo-sciences were dancing a wild gavotte with religion and actual science, weather-watchers took a deep dive in another direction. The sun and the moon, they said, the planets and the stars, that's what governed the weather. These weren't eccentrics, but the scientific elite of the Renaissance. (To be fair, it probably seemed no less nuts to them than the moon governing the tides, but that doesn't make them any less wrong.) An 'astrometeorologist' would monitor eclipses or planetary conjunctions and use them to predict the weather, often years ahead, publishing their findings in hotly anticipated almanacs. Johannes Stöffler, for example, very much a man of his time, confidently foresaw a world-ending deluge a quarter of a century into the future. People took to the hills. The Great Flood of 1524, needless to say, did not come.

The steady creep of empiricism, however, finally put paid to all that. People started to look, to measure, to record, to analyse, to work outwards from the facts, all of which became easier with the invention of accurate and affordable instruments, especially thermometers and barometers.* Once you had a reliable way to measure air pressure, it was hard not to notice that it held higher and steadier in good weather, fell before bad weather, and that the faster the fall, the worse the weather, the stronger the wind. This knowledge, then, allowed us to start issuing warnings of our own, rather than relying on divine intervention.

Weather mattered on land, but it mattered even more at sea. Seafarers, whether naval officers or merchantmen, were heavily invested in understanding the weather, which made them necessary pioneers of scrupulous record-keeping.

---

* It was a pupil of Galileo who, in seventeenth-century Italy, shucked off another Aristotelian misconception: that air had no weight. Evangelista Torricelli proved not only that it did, but that you could *measure* it, using the height of a column of water or, even better, a column of mercury, in a vacuum. At the time, his neighbours thought his fledgling barometers were a bit witchy, but soon even the God-fearing Defoe had one. During the Great Storm, the mercury fell so low he assumed his kids had messed with it.

In a ship's log, every hour, you noted down, then as now, the wind speed, the wind direction and a barometer reading, meaning it was easy to check back and see what the weather was doing on a given day, at a given latitude and longitude. Put dozens, then hundreds, then thousands, then tens of thousands of logbooks together, and you started to be able to spot patterns. You could be pretty sure that the wind backed (i.e. moved anti-clockwise) before a depression and veered (i.e. moved clockwise) after it. You could be pretty sure where the trade winds were waiting. You could be pretty sure when the hurricane season started. In the Age of Sail this was vital information.

It is, therefore, no surprise that it was a naval man in a maritime economy who took weather analysis to the next level. Vice-Admiral Robert FitzRoy was, above all, a crack seaman, the first person to get full marks on the gruelling exams to pass from midshipman to lieutenant. He was a devout Christian, a deeply moral man. He was depressive and had a temper. In his twenties, he was given command of a round-the-world surveying trip, which lasted from 1831 to 1836. Hankering after educated company on the voyage, he offered a young graduate called Charles Darwin a spot as a naturalist on the *Beagle* – with the consequences we all know so well. By his late forties, though, FitzRoy's career was in the doldrums after he'd made a hash of governing

New Zealand: he'd had the unenviable job of trying to mediate between Maoris and land-hungry settlers. He was, however, offered a second act.

In 1854, he hustled hard for the job of meteorological statist at the new Meteorological Department of the Board of Trade, which would see him compiling and scrutinising maritime weather data.* But he decided to go one better. He wouldn't only tell ship captains what had happened in the past. He would tell them what might happen in the future. This was radical stuff. In fact, the suggestion that we might be able to *forecast* (even the word itself was relatively new) rather than merely record the weather, provoked gales of laughter in parliament.

But FitzRoy was nothing if not determined. He knew falling pressure meant bad weather. He knew bad weather tracked west to east. If barometers were plummeting in westerly PLYMOUTH, wouldn't naval cutters and packet ships and fishing smacks in easterly THAMES like to know? Until that decade, it would have been impossible to get word from one end of the country to the other fast

---

* It's interesting how geopolitical wind-shifts have shunted the Met Office between different government departments. The mid-nineteenth century was full-throttle *Pax Britannica*, so understanding the weather was all about improving the safety and journey times – and profits – of merchant ships. Come the dicier twentieth century, the Met Office migrated first to the Air Ministry, then to the Ministry of Defence. It now sits inside the Department for Science, Innovation and Technology.

enough, but a new piece of information technology, the electric telegraph – 'superficial, sudden, unsifted, too fast for the truth', warned the *New York Times*; *plus ça change* – would make FitzRoy's warnings possible.

FitzRoy, armed with his weather charts, which collated data from all around Britain and Ireland, now possessed what he called 'an eye in space', which allowed him to look down on the whole North Atlantic. A god's eye view, in fact: he styled them 'synoptic charts', an homage to the synoptic, i.e. 'seeing all at once', gospels of Matthew, Mark and Luke.

A national disaster, as so often happens, gave his plans added impetus. On the night of 25–6 October 1859, a passenger ship called the *Royal Charter*, returning home to Liverpool from Australia, was wrecked. Four hundred and fifty people died. The ship had passed Holyhead in the afternoon and continued north, hugging a dangerous lee shore, with night coming on, with the weather rapidly deteriorating, with no pilot, for the sake (in the words of an outraged contemporary newspaper report) 'of saving a few hours at the close of an astonishingly rapid and successful passage'. Storm winds drove the *Royal Charter* aground off Anglesey. The ship started to break up. A Maltese sailor, attached to a rope, managed (astonishingly) to swim ashore, allowing the horrified onlookers to haul a lucky few back to land. Only 41 people survived. No women. No children.

The shipwreck, part national tragedy, part national disgrace, was a news event so large that Charles Dickens himself bustled west to hoover up mawkish local colour; for FitzRoy, it meant that he was given the go-ahead to trial his weather warnings. Thirteen telegraph stations ringed Britain and Ireland at (to follow the path of today's *Shipping Forecast*) Aberdeen, Berwick, Hull, Yarmouth, Dover, Portsmouth, Jersey, Plymouth, Penzance, Cork, Galway, Londonderry and Greenock. These stations zapped weather info to FitzRoy in his office in London at 0900 every morning. He'd draw up his charts, read the runes and, if necessary, zap back a gale warning by coffee-time. To alert mariners, he also devised a basic system of cones and drums, different combinations to be hoisted for different wind directions, which were easily visible from land and sea. It was all very Victorian (in a good way): principled, ambitious, scientific.

On 6 February 1861, his first weather warning went out: a gale on the northeast coast. All went according to plan. The gale arrived. The cones worked – *if* you saw them, *if* you obeyed them. Some skippers at South Shields pooh-poohed the cones and were wrecked. Whitby had no telegraph warning, so had no cones. Twelve lifeboat-men drowned within sight of the town, having rescued five boatloads of foundering fishermen. As Peter Moore writes

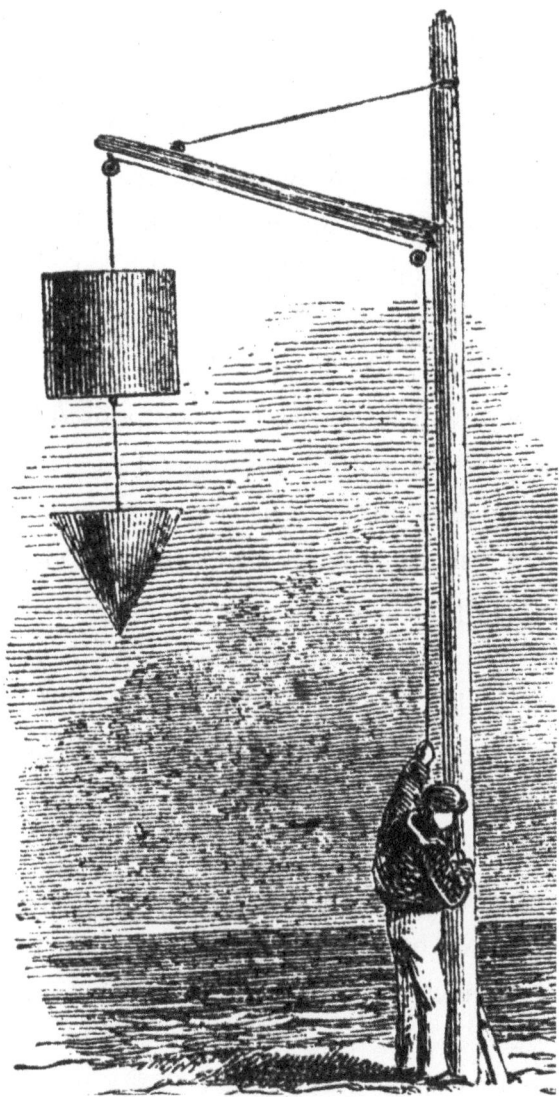

in *The Weather Experiment*, a brilliant account of meteorological advances in the nineteenth century, seaman had to learn to trust FitzRoy. 'It was a problem,' he writes, 'of faith more than anything else. People had to believe the science.' Incidentally, on Sundays there were no observations, no charts, no warnings. On the Lord's day, the weather remained firmly in the lap of the god(s).*

Nevertheless, that first warning of gales in what we'd now call FORTH, TYNE and HUMBER was judged a massive success. A leader in the *Times* praised FitzRoy's perspicacity, which in 1861 was as good an endorsement as you were going to get. The stage was set for expansion. More telegraph stations were added. More ports received his tip-offs. And six months later, his forecasts even started to appear in the newspapers. Again, they were a hit. Who didn't want to be able to see into the future? Certainly, Queen Victoria did: she sent messengers round to FitzRoy's house, asking for a personalised forecast for WIGHT, where she used to staycation.

That moment, FitzRoy waving off the messengers, their silken breeches sparkling in the sunshine, his proud family clustering round him, 'Papa, oh Papa, were they

---

* Nowadays, if you linger in bed after Sunday's 0520 forecast, rather than getting washed and dressed for early communion, you are treated to *Bells on Sunday*. God, very thoughtfully, comes to you.

really from the queen?' is (pretend this is a biopic) the high point of the third act. It's the beat where, after all his travails, he's finally made it. Sadly, FitzRoy's story is a tragedy, which means, in the next frame, it all starts to unravel. As he shepherds his over-excited children back to the breakfast room for their tea and kippers – *whump* – a book tied up in brown paper lands on his doormat. The past, you see, has come back to haunt him.

In 18—,* his old shipmate Charles Darwin finally published *On the Origin of Species*, his explosive theory of evolution, grown from seeds planted aboard the *Beagle*. FitzRoy, along with his late lamented first wife, was a literal-minded Christian, and was appalled at the unwitting role he'd played in facilitating the birth of this heretical tract. Explains Moore: 'if *Origin* was scientific trespass on the past, on ground that had been held for a millennium by the Church, then logically the forecasts he had in mind would mean trespassing into the divine future. Forecast and evolution were scientific twins.'

Worse was to come. Public opinion as we know, spins like a weathercock. FitzRoy's name was so closely associated with his forecasts that it didn't take long for *Punch* magazine and other satirists to start cracking jokes when he

---

* I'm blurring the timeline, but this is a movie after all.

called it wrong. He couldn't nail down the science behind his forecasts. The Board of Trade wasn't convinced it was getting its money's worth. His budgets were cut at work. He had his own money worries at home. Worn out, worn down, his health failing, he died by suicide in 1865. Not long afterwards, his forecasts were axed.

But then, in a moving posthumous fifth act, people started to write to the newspapers telling them how FitzRoy had saved their lives. The RNLI couldn't praise him enough. The maritime establishment wanted his warnings back. (Although down where I live in the West Country, we were apparently less enthusiastic. Bad weather hits us first, so our geography doomed us to be the dutiful warn-ers, not the lucky warn-ees.) The resuscitated warnings later moved from telegraph to radio, with a first iteration of the *Shipping Forecast* launching in 1924, before debuting on the BBC in 1925. And today, as we'll read more about in MAPS, the largest forecast area is named FITZROY in his honour.

When we hear a gale warning nowadays, our response is conditioned by a cultural moment which predates the Victorian era, but whose influence we still feel very strongly today. Why, when we know storms are so perilous, why are we drawn towards them? Why do we stand on clifftops oohing and aahing at crashing waves? Why do we watch *The Perfect Storm*, *The Day After Tomorrow*, *2012*, even when the plots blow cyclonically? Why do some of us even choose to race yachts through the Southern Ocean, where force 8 is *nothing*? The answer is that, like it or not, we're all heirs to the Romantic imagination.

We weren't always storm-chasers. John Ruskin, Victorian thought leader *extraordinaire*, points out that in 'The Man of Law's Tale', Geoffrey Chaucer sends his character, the beautiful Lady Constance, on any number of medieval maritime misadventures, 'but neither he nor his audience appear to be capable of receiving any sensation, but one of simple aversion, from waves, ships, or sands'. Back then, a storm-tossed sea was simply awful; the Romantics needed to get their teeth into us before it could become *awe*-ful as well. Witness, for example, the travel writer Eric Newby rounding Cape Horn in the 1930s on board one of the last great sail-powered merchant ships. Confronted by the overwhelming might of the waves, he felt nothing more or less than 'certain of the existence of an infinitely powerful and at the same time merciful God'.

Lord Byron, whose grandfather 'Foul-Weather Jack' set a round-the-world speed record, found no such 'terror' in a breaking sea, but rather a 'pleasing fear': 'Roll on, thou deep and dark blue Ocean – roll! / Ten thousand fleets sweep over thee in vain; / Man marks the earth with ruin – his control / Stops with the shore[.]' Our inner Romantic, you see, loves to ponder how our delusions of grandeur, our wave-ruling facade, can be smashed to smithereens with one swipe of the West Wind's paw. A proud ship, explains Ruskin, breasting the waves under full sail, is an unworthy subject. A ruined ship, on the other hand, be it ever so tattered and torn, is not merely picturesque, but also *noble*, because it allows 'man' to 'meditate upon Fate as it conquers his work', which is much better than sitting back and admiring the work itself.

Jane Austen, though, whose brothers fought in the Napoleonic Wars that lurk, shark-like, beneath the surface of her novels, had as little time as (I imagine) Foul-Weather Jack did for young popinjays who glamorised the sea from a safe distance. Charlotte, heroine of Austen's unfinished work, *Sanditon*, finds herself cornered by just such a man, one Sir Edward Denham, a florid berk in full spate. He covers the terrific grandeur of the ocean's storms, the deep fathoms of its abysses, its quick vicissitudes, its direful deceptions, its gulls and samphire, until, notes the satiric narrator, 'he began to stagger her by the number of his quotations and the bewilderment of some of his sentences.' Another deluded youth (me), after literally nearly drowning her best girlfriends off the west coast of the United States (the forecast said the wind'd top out at 8; we got 10) wrote in *Yachting Monthly*: 'I will always get my kicks in big seas on dark nights.'

It takes a writer with the wit of the late, great Jonathan Raban (himself a passionate sailor) to put bozos like me in our place. People who started to venture offshore for pleasure, he wrote in his introduction to *The Oxford Book of the Sea*, flattered themselves that they were braving a quasi-biblical wilderness, 'a palace of hardship and voluntary suffering', a place where fantasies of 'romantic sublimity' consorted with 'the idea that the sea is a kind of alembic, created by God as an instrument for testing the resolution of the British character'.

Putting out to sea always involves balancing risk and reward, whether the reward you're chasing is victory in battle, a hold stuffed with fish, a faster passage than your commercial rivals, or your own good time. Great mariners – and great maritime fiction – must strike the right balance between caution and bravado. There's triumph when Patrick O'Brian's Lucky Jack Aubrey makes yet another bold call; there's near-tragedy when the captain in Conrad's novella, *Typhoon*, refuses to heed a falling barometer.

When my brother and I were growing up, although our family subscribed to no organised religion, we did pay obeisance to one household god: the *prudent mariner*. Clad in dripping oilskins, s/he loomed large over our childhood, invoked and propitiated. S/he it was who presided over my parents' nuptials, who baptised us with binnacle polish and pollock guts, who kept us safe, whether we were fishing a wintry PLYMOUTH dawn or quote-unquote summering in the *Shipping Forecast*'s northern quadrant, FAIR ISLE '89, NORTH UTSIRE '90, SOUTHEAST ICELAND '91.

In Britain today, though, we have a firm expectation that we shouldn't be caught out. We feel it's the forecasters' job to keep us safe, and we're disappointed, even angry, when they don't. The Great Storm of 1987, with its hurricane-force winds, blew across the south of England overnight from 15–16 October, killing 18 people. (The number would have been much higher had it struck during the day.) The storm caused a billion pounds' worth of damage, including the irreparable loss of millions of mature trees. Infamously, we blamed Michael Fish, the mild and moustachioed face of the weather gods inside the Met Office, for not giving us a clear warning.

In 1987, the Met Office was juggling perhaps 1,200 observations every 24 hours. But while that would have felt luxurious to FitzRoy, it's nothing compared with today's 215 billion observations, processed by a monster supercomputer. At the same time, manned weather-ships, which had long provided detailed intel about incoming depressions, were being phased out, while the satellite and weather-buoy technology that went on to replace them was still in its infancy. So although the Met Office knew bad weather was coming, it thought the depression would barely clip the south coast – and it certainly failed to predict quite how ballistic the winds would be.

There are terrifying accounts of ferries and a container ship caught at sea, forced to stand off Channel ports which the storm had made much too dangerous to enter. But perhaps the most disturbing story of all is that of the *Earl William*, an old ferry moored in Harwich, doing service as a floating immigration detention centre. Its existence angered people across the political spectrum in much the same way it might now. Many were horrified. Others wondered why 'queue-jumpers' had been given such a cushy berth. On board that night were dozens of asylum-seekers, many of them Tamils who were fleeing Sinhalese violence in Sri Lanka; violence which had roots, amongst other things, in how the Tamils were perceived to have been favoured under British colonial rule. When the storm hit, it broke the ferry's mooring-lines, sending it careering across the Stour Estuary where, thankfully, it grounded on a mud bank. It was a close shave. Seriously shaken, the government ended their detention. A Tamil rights campaigner called it 'the furious hand of nature'. The academic Robin Cohen, author of *Frontiers of Identity*, an exploration of Britishness, writes: 'There did, indeed, seem to be some message given from on high.'*

$$\dagger$$

The irony, so sledgehammer-unsubtle it's perfect for a Hollywood screenplay: Defoe and co. were sort of right all along. When it comes to *climate* (as opposed to weather), it *is* all our fault. We thought we were doing what the Christian God wanted, growing and growing, bigger better faster more, being fruitful and increasing in number and filling the earth and subduing it and ruling over the fish and the birds and every living creature. Turns out we might have misheard.

Demonstrating outside a Labour Party conference at Brighton in 2019, climate activists XR, loved and loathed for their direct-action protests, wheeled a massive light-vessel along the seafront, foghorns blaring, delivering its

---

* There were other gods at work that October: the invisible hand of the market. The London Stock Exchange, which traditionally only shuts for world wars, didn't open on Friday 16 October. When it re-opened on Monday, the market unexpectedly crashed – you'll know it as Black Monday. Why it happened remains as inexplicable to us as the Great Storm was to Daniel Defoe.

own version of the *Shipping Forecast*: 'VIKING, NORTH UTSIRE, severe gales, summer heatwaves … moderate or poor, becoming desperate soon.' Climate change is real. Scientists, thousands upon thousands of FitzRoys all across the globe, are showing us their data, over and over again. Some people in some parliaments are still laughing. Some people, like the captain of *Royal Charter*, are sticking to their schedule, ploughing on regardless. Some – short-sighted? – people are crossing their fingers that our islands' temperate (i.e. dank and drizzly) climate will help us weather the worst. But as we'll see in MAPS and CROSSINGS, the idea of fortress Britain, a little world apart, moated by water, walled by weather, lies somewhere between fiction and fantasy.

MAPS

Oh, it's a snug little island!

An eighteenth-century patriotic banger

A T THE DAWN OF THIS CENTURY, Robert FitzRoy, the
star of our last chapter, made a surprise return to the
headlines. The Met Office, his baby now all grown up, had
agreed with our neighbours along the Atlantic seaboard
to co-ordinate the names of everyone's maritime forecast
areas. Spain had a Finisterre. We had FINISTERRE.
They weren't in quite the same place. The Met Office
ceded the name, which after all does refer to a famous and
indisputably very *Spanish* headland, and offered to come
up with a new name instead, plumping rather touchingly
for FITZROY.

But this piece of humdrum meteorological house-
keeping was characterised (by some) as nothing more or
less than an act of craven capitulation, as if we'd fought
the Armada all over again and lost. Sure, it was a bit of a
confected media kerfuffle, but there was still a deluge of
letters and articles, joking/not-joking that the Spanish

would be coming for Gibraltar next.* A *Guardian* satirist said any British citizenship test should include the question: What would make you angry enough to write to your MP? a) British involvement in an illegal war, b) arms sales to dictators – or c) giving up Finisterre. Frankly, said the *Times*, it'd be less controversial to change the LBW rule.

The reaction, explains Kate Fox in her sharp study, *Watching the English*, shouldn't surprise us: 'the weather may be one of the few things about which the English are still unselfconsciously and unashamedly patriotic.' The weather, she says, is a prop and stay, a bright buoyed channel leading safely through the jagged rocks of small talk. At the time, 'foreigners' told her they were bewildered by the Finisterre debacle. An American exclaimed: 'Anyone would think they'd tried to change the words of the Lord's Prayer!' But that only showed how little he knew about the foibles of his adopted land.

No religion is fast gaining ground on Christianity in the UK; indeed, it was the most popular box to tick at the last census in both Scotland and Wales. And yet, putting personal beliefs aside, religion has historically fostered

---

* The Spanish Met Office is still trolling us, btw. Their forecast area that covers the Western Approaches to the Channel is called Gran Sol, which I can only make mean Big Sun. This seems ... ironic?

community, a sense of belonging. At its best, it helps people come together, to feel their differences washed away by something bigger and better than themselves. Absent a shared faith in a god up there, keeping his weather eye on us, we can turn to the radio for a sense of togetherness. Carol Ann Duffy, the former poet laureate, knew how everybody felt when she rhymed 'Darkness outside. Inside, the radio's prayer' with 'Rockall. Malin. Dogger. Finisterre.' (What on earth would she have rhymed FitzRoy with? The radio's – *ahoy*???) When the *Shipping Forecast* calls its names, it *is* like a little prayer; in the midnight hour, we *do* feel its power.*

The celebrated nature writer, Richard Mabey, also tuned in to this spiritual frequency. 'Weather forecasters,' he wrote, 'have become our new shamans, and the forecast has, in a sense, become *part* of the weather, an affecting, emotional experience as well as a detached prediction.' When we exchange meteorological commonplaces such as 'turned out nice again', we are acknowledging that, superficially different though we might be, we share a *common place*. We are all, he says, in it, in the weather, together.

The *Shipping Forecast*, then, creates a broad, ecumenical community of listeners, who know they are listening as

---

* Footnote for my parents: this is a reference to a very famous Madonna song.

one. Alongside those invisible others, we embark on what Alexandra Harris, in her riveting study *Weatherland*, calls 'an imaginary offshore tour'. Once we're safely aboard, 'Cold headlands appear, unvisited beaches, moving lights on black swell, a low groan and clang from a container ship, discs and dials in a small cabin, a flickering screen.' Together, we can contemplate the unknown.

But you can, if you're so minded, slam the tiller hard over and try a totally different tack. You can turn this tucked-up cosiness on its head. The *Shipping Forecast*, after all, is the child of the armed forces. Fathered by a vice-admiral, its nursery was the Air Ministry, its school the Ministry of Defence. From that point of view, the *Shipping Forecast* is no lullaby, no cradle song, but a bugle, a reveille, summoning His Majesty's subjects to a sort of maritime march-past, which beats the bounds of Englishness, of Britishness, of UsNess. It belongs (to borrow Professor John Brannigan's more academic phraseology) 'to the imperial discourse of sea power' and is an 'attempt to master oceanic space'.

Exhibit A. After the 0048 forecast wraps up, what do you hear? 'God Save the King'. Exhibit B. For most of my lifetime, what accompanied the dawn forecast? The 'UK Theme', an instrumental mash-up of sentimental airs, which segued around the four nations, braced up with a dollop of 'What Shall We Do with the Drunken Sailor?' and a dash of 'Rule Britannia'.*

Professor Alison Light also explores this idea, remembering how when she was growing up, the *Shipping Forecast* meshed with 'the powerful threads of a nationalism which tied my sense of self umbilically to Englishness'. As a child, waiting for *Listen with Mother*, she knew that when the wireless said WIGHT, it meant her, her family, their friends. It meant the sea shanties she sang at primary school; it meant the Still & West, the Lord Nelson, the Captain's Table, the Portsmouth pubs groaning with maritime trinkets.

But what is fascinating, and part of the *Shipping Forecast*'s genius, is that just as you think you've landed it in a net labelled nationalism, it spits out the hook, and slips and slithers back into the sea. Think of the map. Of the 31 areas, fewer than half touch a shore which could be conceivably called British, let alone English, a tacit acknowledgement that our borders, since we've had any concept of borders, have backed and veered all over the place.

---

* *Huge* plaudits to the *Today* programme pranksters who announced on April Fool's Day 2006, the year the 'UK Theme' left the airwaves, that it was to be replaced by an 'EU Theme'.

Who 'we' think 'we' are has boxed the compass, sometimes anchored on the island of Britain, sometimes sailing away north, south, east or west across the not-so-sundering sea. We've been a northwest frontier province of the Roman Empire; the southern outpost of a Nordic conglomerate; the western flank of an Anglo-French joint enterprise; an offshore Protestant pariah in a world of continental Catholic superpowers; the centre of a vast empire with TIME itself running through the Greenwich meridian; and, until recently, the reluctant outlier of a phantasmagorical European superstate. When the *Shipping Forecast* debuted a hundred years ago, it was broadcast from the smoggy, foggy heart of the British Empire, which was then, having just accepted the secession of the majority of Ireland, only five years past its territorial peak. A hundred years later, empire is a busted flush and the Republic of Ireland is part of a European Union, which we fought to enter – and to leave. In fact, the UK *qua* the UK is actually three years younger than the *Shipping Forecast*, which makes our current borders froth, foam, spray, spume on the waves of time.

At the risk of derailing our *amour propre*, for the majority of the 5,000+ years of civilised, i.e. city-building, human history, we've basically been hanging out with the scaly monsters at the edge of the map. Amy Jeffs, in her lovely collection of tales from our islands' mythology, *Storyland*, explains: 'To live in Britain then was to possess an edginess, a brinkhood, unknown to the great eastern citizens whose homes occupied the centre of the map.' We appear in recorded history as a rumour. Phoenician traders, originally from the Mediterranean coast of what is now Lebanon and Syria, sailed west through the Pillars of Hercules and turned north, possibly as far as Britain, seeking the tidy profits which could be made from the backwards, but resource-rich, Atlantic fringe. The Greek sailor Pytheas – who, Columbus-like, discovered us for civilisation – sailed even further north, coming home with tall tales of midnight suns and frozen oceans. Some of his readers thought it was all a pack of lies; after all, said the geographer Strabo, *nowhere* was colder and grimmer than Britain, except possibly, he granted, Ireland.

Two thousand years ago, though, we had our first walk-on role on the world stage. Julius Caesar came, saw and sailed away. The Emperor Claudius came, saw and stayed. For 350 years, we were Rome's rough-and-ready, heavily militarised frontier. In their eyes we were, as the narrator of Joseph Conrad's *Heart of Darkness* ponders while sitting on a boat in the Thames Estuary, 'one of the dark places of the earth'. The Romans (itself a baggy word; the Romans stationed here came from across Europe, the

Middle East and North Africa) exploited southern and eastern Britain for farmland (our wheat and beef fed the armies of the Rhine), for raw materials (you can find Mendip lead in Pompeii), for furs, for hunting dogs, for people to enslave. We were rude and barbarous. We were, according to a Latin slur found on a wooden tablet near Hadrian's Wall, *Brittunculi*.

When Rome, declining and falling, quit Britain, we fell off the map again. We were raided from the west by people from Ireland, who were confusingly called Scotti. We were raided from the east by people from the Netherlands, Germany and Denmark, who were called Angles and Saxons and Jutes. And just when we (whoever exactly 'we' were by then) thought we could relax, we were raided from the north by people from Denmark, Sweden and Norway, who were called Vikings. They started off sacking rich monasteries and terrorising coastal and river-ine communities, before gradually colonising large chunks of the middle and north of England. Alfred the Great, king of the Anglo-Saxons,* held the line, preventing the

---

* There is, FYI, a niche culture war being fought over whether *Anglo-Saxon* is the correct shorthand for the Germanic tribes who went on to form the first English kingdoms – or an inherently racist term which needs to be retired. If we were academics, we'd probably have to pick a side, but I think we can tiptoe backwards out of the debate, sticking to common (and indeed their own) usage until everyone's made up their minds.

Vikings from overrunning the south and west – until, that is, Danish Cnut overwhelmed Anglo-Saxon Edmund Ironside, and England was absorbed into what (some) historians call the North Sea Empire, which existed from 1013 to 1042.

We think of the next great redrawing of the map – 1066 – as England vs France, or at least England vs Normandy, but it was actually the culmination of decades of Viking-adjacent scraps. On the 'English' side was Harold Godwinson, who had Danish heritage via his mother. On the other side was a) William the Bastard, soon to be Conqueror, whose great-great-great-grandfather was a Viking who'd decamped to Normandy,* and b) Harald Hardrada, a bona fide Viking, king of Norway, hard as nails, minted after a stint in Constantinople, who fancied he could resurrect the North Sea Empire. Harold G marched north, defeated Harald H at Stamford Bridge, marched back south – and was defeated by William B at Hastings.

What followed was a radical southeastward expansion of our mental map, towards Normandy, towards France. For centuries afterwards, the 'English' aristocracy spoke French, married French aristocrats and had lands

---

* A Norman, after all, is literally a North man, a Norse man, a Viking.

in France. The 1152 marriage of Henry II of England and Eleanor of Aquitaine, whose power base was on the French Atlantic coast, paved the way for a cross-BISCAY entity (you can argue the toss whether it was an empire, a commonwealth or a composite monarchy), which covered England, bits of Ireland and Wales and *half* of France. How much of France was English ebbed and flowed for the next four hundred years, until the French finally booted us out of Calais in 1558.

Us? Well, *some* of us. We're running the risk of being dangerously south/east/English-centric. If you lived in Orkney, FAIR ISLE or Shetland, after 1066 you remained very much part of the ex-Viking, Norse orbit. In the fifteenth century, for example, the islands were briefly part of the Kalmar Union, a Scandinavian power bloc. Even when they were ceded to Scotland (after the family of a Danish princess failed to cough up her dowry), they kept some distinctive legal rights, called Udal law. During the Second World War, fishing boats ferried refugees from Nazi-occupied Norway to safety in Shetland, returning with British secret agents and supplies for the resistance, a clandestine operation known as the Shetland Bus. Leafing through my dad's account of a pit-stop we made in Lerwick in the nineties, I found the route was still popular: 'We tied up alongside a Lofoten-bound yacht, the only Brit in the harbour; the rest were Norwegian booze-cruisers.'

It is, of course, equally important to remember that the Romans never conquered Cornwall, Wales, Scotland or the island of Ireland – nor did the Anglo-Saxons. The Normans had a crack at Wales, but England didn't fully annexe it for another three hundred years. The Vikings mopped up a lot of Scottish islands, but not Scotland itself. And Scotland was none of England's business (despite England's best efforts) until a Scottish king inherited the English throne after the death of Elizabeth I. The Vikings had a toehold in Ireland, but never took over; it was the Normans and Tudors who did the conquering and colonis-ing, with Oliver Cromwell and William of Orange fighting to stay in the teeth of increasingly trenchant opposition.

Today, we sometimes bracket together those current and former parts of the United Kingdom – the parts that aren't and have never been English – by calling them Celtic. But that term, which harks back to pre-Roman tribes who lived across a broad swathe of western Europe, was only popularised in the eighteenth century, and then only to refer to a language family. Certainly, it had no mean-ing back when England was trying to forge its mini-empire across the islands of Britain and Ireland. The Scottish historian Neal Ascherson tells us that expressions like the

'Celtic nations' and the 'Celtic Fringe' are really English statements about England, a way to describe people the English saw as Other. 'The main thing', he writes, 'that those Atlantic nations and communities have in common is not Celticity. It's their experience of English expansion.'

For centuries, then, the very idea of 'us' as an island race, alone, unique, distinct would have been patently absurd. What's more, the water around Britain wasn't a bulwark, a barricade. It was criss-crossed by rulers, merchants, brides, artisans, armies; after all, until the railways, it was often much easier to travel by sea than land. Ask Geoffrey Chaucer's Shipman, ranging happily across the *Shipping Forecast*'s capacious map: 'Fro Gootlond to the cape of Fynystere, / And every cryke in Britaigne and in Spayne'. Michael Pye, in *The Edge of the World*, a brilliant study of our relationship with the North Sea, sums it up very well: 'Our very separate identity,' he writes, 'turns out to be an error, even a lie.'

What changed? What launched the whole sceptred-isle drawbridge-up white-cliffs-down schtick? *Babies*. Henry VIII needed a (legitimate) son. Catherine of Aragon gave him a daughter. He also 'needed' Anne Boleyn, which meant he needed a divorce. The Pope said no. He did it anyway. The consequence, which came as the Reformation was sweeping across northern Europe, was our severance from Rome and Catholicism, which had so long tied us to a common European 'Christendom'. 'This spiritual isolation,' Norman Davies writes in his addictive history, *The Isles*, 'was arguably more profound than anything that resulted from all the political invasions and geographical changes since the Ice Age.'

But there was another big bone of contention between us and the maritime powers of Europe: empire. Religious rupture coincided with the era of maritime exploration and imperial expansion, which was originally pioneered by the Spanish, the Portuguese and the Dutch. We watched our rivals jealously, disrupting and harrying them when we could, before eventually challenging and finally surpassing them. The men who cut such a dash defending England against the Spanish Armada (coming up next in CROSSINGS) were, in fact, the very same men who helped England take its first steps towards its overseas empire – including our earliest involvement in the trade in enslaved Africans. From tentative Tudor beginnings, our imperial ambitions grew and grew until, by the Victorian era, our mental map stretched far, far beyond the *Shipping Forecast*'s more modest bounds. Like a monomaniacal child slapping hotels on Park Lane and Mayfair, we assured ourselves, and anyone else who'd listen, that the British Empire was the biggest and the best. But because we liked to think we were Christian and civilised and wise and just, we also took pains to assure our imperial subjects that they weren't *them* – on the contrary, they were *us*.

After the Second World War, 1,027 men and women (plus two stowaways) disembarked from the *Empire Windrush* at Tilbury Docks in THAMES, putting that assurance to the test. The majority of those on board had travelled from Jamaica, Bermuda, Trinidad and British Guiana, all part of the British Empire, and included more than a hundred serving and former members of the Armed Forces. When they left their homes and families, they thought they were coming to the Mother Country, a place where they, so they'd been told, belonged. But once they were actually here, we told them, or rather we told *us*, 'Aaah, *terribly* sorry, our mistake, you're not actually *us* after all.' The upshot has been decades of racism, structural and casual, covert and overt; successive legislation to restrict further immigration; and the 'hostile environment' of the 2010s, which was supposed to target illegal immigration but ended up harming *us*, British people, people who were born here, people who belonged. The Windrush generation, as dedicated reporting has shown us, was sold a lie.

Back in 24 CE, we were a hairy irrelevance, the butt of our sophisticated neighbours' jokes. In 1924, we'd spent a generation thinking we were the mighty all-conquering sun about which the world turned. Come 2024, we're still puzzling out where exactly we might fit between those two poles.

When the *Shipping Forecast* reached its half-century, we experimented with one possible answer: we stretched out our hand across the Channel and joined the European Economic Community, which became the European Union, only to snatch our hand back in the referendum, saying it had been a mistake. I don't know whether that 47-year experiment in economic and political union will, five hundred years hence, seem as quaint as the Kalmar Union, or whether it's Brexit itself that'll be seen as the quixotic hiccup. Only time will tell.

Until we come up with a satisfactory answer to that and many other questions, why not, as we drift off to sleep, CROMARTYFORTHTYNE dream of a new cartography? A cartography that WIGHTPORTLAND-PLYMOUTH embraces everyone who lives on these islands. Let's dream that every single man, woman and child LUNDYFASTNETIRISHSEA is safe and warm at 0048 when the *Shipping Forecast* sounds, whether they're the tiny few listening for business, the denizens of Radio

4-land listening for pleasure, or all the many millions MALINHEBRIDESBAILEY who have never even heard of it, but who are tickled by the swash of radio's waves just the same.

After all, from the *Shipping Forecast*'s point of view, we are not the United Kingdom of Great Britain and Northern Ireland. We are not England, Ireland, Scotland, Wales. We are not Iceland, Norway, Germany, the Netherlands, Belgium, France, Spain, Portugal or Morocco. We are all but the humble subjects of the West Wind.

CROSSINGS

The prostrating experiences of foreigners between Calais and Dover have always been an agreeable side to English prepossessions.

Robert Louis Stevenson, 'The English Admirals' (1881)

IMAGINE ALL THE WANNABE INVADERS who've stood with one foot on their ship, one foot on the shore. Imagine them screwing up their eyes and staring across the waters. Imagine them begging their god(s) for a hint, a sign, *something* to tell them whether the weather would hold – or whether the tide of history would turn against them. Julius Caesar, William the Conqueror, Philip of Spain, William of Orange, Napoleon Bonaparte, Adolf Hitler, they'd all have given their eye-teeth for a *Shipping Forecast*. For they all knew, despite their military might, that when it came to crossing the Channel, it was the West Wind who held the balance of power.

To begin at the very beginning, the first people who crossed to Britain were palaeolithic hunter-gatherers. They – oh, they didn't need the *Shipping Forecast*. Forty thousand years ago, we weren't an island. They could just *walk* across. In fact, if you expand 'people' to include

H. neanderthalensis and *H. heidelbergensis,* humans of one stripe or another have been making their way here on foot – ice cover and sea level willing – for pushing a million years.

Neolithic famers, then, were the first people who had no choice but to come by sea. Six thousand years ago, Britain was the final stop on the line of what had been a generations-long mass migration across Europe from Anatolia – and it's thanks to what archaeologists can read in the remnants of those very same eye-teeth that we can be so sure they crossed at all. They brought agriculture with them, which is a very big thing to have carried in (presumably) very small boats. We have no record what the 'native' hunter-gatherers made of the farmers' arrival, nor what the farmers made of the Bronze-Age people who followed them. (Although, seeing as the new 'Beaker' people were better at making weapons and favoured graves celebrating their high-status dead, we can perhaps hazard a guess.) Instead, we'll fast-forward to 55 BCE, the twilight of the Iron Age, when a keen-eyed long-haired fur-clad blue-tattooed young Briton (poetic licence) spotted a massive Roman oarship prowling up and down DOVER.

This boat, captained by a man called Gaius Volusenus, was under orders from Julius Caesar, who'd butchered his way from the Alps to the Channel, to scope out an invasion route. That accomplished, the fleet waited for what they thought was a weather window (*mwah-ha-haaa*) and put to sea. At first, all went according to plan. The footsoldiers, after some undignified thrashing about in heavy armour in the shallows, made it ashore. The transports carrying the cavalry were right behind them when (according to JC's no. 1 bestselling war memoirs) 'so great a storm suddenly arose that none of them could hold their course at sea'. Some ships, he said, were blown east, back the way they'd come; some ships were blown west, in entirely the opposite direction. That might sound contradictory, until you realise this is actually the first ever example in recorded history of that *Shipping Forecast* classic: DOVER, cyclonic 5 to 6, increasing 7 or gale 8, occasionally severe gale 9 later in west. How the watching Britons cheered!

It wasn't only the wind that was on their side, but the tides too. That very same night, the *silly* Romans, used to the Mediterranean's *piddly* rise and fall, were busted by the biggest tides of the month. And since the Channel's full-moon spring tides, then as now, land in the middle of the night, the Romans were caught on the hop. The ships they'd blithely parked on the beach at low tide were swamped. The ships they'd parked at sea dragged their anchors.* It was carnage. Julius Caesar didn't fancy spending winter on hairy-scary Britain with inadequate food, damaged ships, and none of the trappings of civilisation. He scuttled back to Gaul for the winter, tried again, not much more successfully, the following year, and after that the Romans didn't return for a hundred years.

Fast forward to 1066. As discussed in MAPS, the English Viking went north to beat the Hard Viking, while the Norman Viking was mustering his fleet on the southern shore of the Channel, at the mouth of the River Dives. In early September, when Harold G was away fighting Harald H, leaving England's underbelly unprotected, a northerly wind blew, pinning the invaders to the shore. But on 12 September, the West Wind returned from his summer holidays, blew the fleet off its moorings and forced the invaders into the harbour of St Valery, a little further up the coast.

William the Bastard knew what he had to do. According to his chaplain, William of Poitiers, 'he made pious and fervent supplication that the wind which was still adverse might be made favourable to him'. How did he do this? He

---

* If you're a Roman captain who's underestimated the Channel's tidal range, you won't have paid out enough anchor warp. If your warp's too short, your anchor will drag, and bad things will start to happen scarily fast. A dragging anchor was why the Swallows, who didn't mean to go to sea, actually did go to sea in Arthur Ransome's *We Didn't Mean to Go to Sea*.

bade the bones of St Valery be brought forth from their final resting place, and told his soldiers to grovel before them. The saint was impressed! The weathercock at the top of the church tower crrrrreaked, and a disembodied voice murmured DOVER, WIGHT, PORTLAND, south-westerly backing southerly, 3 to 4, fair, good. 'Tumultuously encouraging one another they went on board with the utmost haste,' the chronicle continues, 'and with eager joy began their perilous voyage.' The next morning the fleet landed unopposed at Pevensey in East Sussex, and off they marched to victory.

Fast forward five hundred years. Elizabeth I was on the throne, and the bad guy was Philip II of Spain, meaning this wasn't only a Protestant vs Catholic holy war, but also a family grudge match. Philip was the widowed husband of Mary, Elizabeth's very Catholic half-sister. When Mary died childless, Philip lost no time in proposing to Elizabeth, aiming to bolster Spanish and Catholic influence in England, but the Virgin Queen hummed and hawed long enough that he plumped for a French princess instead. Since then, Philip and Elizabeth had been fighting various proxy wars, with Spain propping up Mary, Queen of Scots, and England propping up rebels in the Netherlands (which, confusingly, was ruled by Spain).

In the summer of 1588, flush with silver pillaged from the Americas, an enormous Spanish fleet, loaded with 19,000 soldiers, was primed to sail to Flanders, aiming to pick up an additional 30,000 battle-hardened troops and deliver them across the Channel to topple Elizabeth. The number of troops England could muster was peanuts in comparison: if the Spanish fleet landed, Elizabeth was toast. Famously, it didn't go according to plan.

The English fleet, most memorably featuring Sir Francis Drake, harried the Armada the length of the Channel. The Spanish anchored off Calais. The English flushed them out with fire-ships. The two fleets squared off to do battle near the small port of Gravelines, then part of the Spanish Netherlands. The *Shipping Forecast* was HUMBER, THAMES, DOVER, south or southwest, 6 to 7, showers, moderate, occasionally very poor. It could have gone either way: the Spanish had more firepower, but the English made better use of the guns they had. Towards the end of a hard day's fighting, a squall hit, and the Spanish wriggled clear of the shallows and stood north. The wind blew strong during the night, and the Armada ran blind before it.* By dawn, it veered northwest (the cold front passing?) which meant the Armada was now making leeway onto the Flemish

---

* Just the thought of this gives me the willies. Even with GPS, lit buoys and an echo-sounder, that stretch of sea is stressful enough.

sandbanks. The Spanish tried to force another engagement but, in the words of Garrett Mattingly's Pulitzer-winning history of the Armada, 'The English were standing by to watch the destruction of their enemies by the hand of God.' The sailor swinging the lead on the Spanish admiral's galleon hit seven fathoms, then six. Continues Mattingly, 'In those minutes every man in the Armada with eyes in his head must have tasted death'. But then, a miracle – for the *Spanish*. The wind backed! No longer was it death-dealing northwest, but hope-proffering west-southwest, giving them the angle they needed to claw their way into deeper water. The Armada was saved ... for now.

But the West Wind did not abandon England in her hour of need. A helping hand from either the North or the East Wind would have allowed the Armada to turn the tables on the English fleet, but our favourite despot confined them both to barracks. Instead, the Spanish had to sail on north, with a southwesterly wind and the English at their backs. Drake and co., eyeing their mouldy stores and leaking water butts, reluctantly decided to put in at FORTH, praying the wind would hold.

Meanwhile, the Spanish found themselves dithering in the cold seas above Scotland, afraid of hitting Orkney or Shetland if they turned west too soon. When they eventually tacked out around the outside of Ireland, the fleet was in a dreadful state: low on food, low on water, low on ammo. Many of the ships were also without anchors, having been forced to 'cut and run' the night the English sent in the fireships. Gales wrecked some Spanish ships. Others foundered when they tried, with neither charts nor pilots, to sneak ashore for supplies. Those who made it to land were often killed by English soldiers, although there are tales of sympathetic Irish Catholics spiriting a lucky few to safety. Half the men who sailed on the Armada did not make it home alive. King Philip, according to a popular anecdote, reacted to this unmitigated disaster with trademark sang-froid: 'I sent my ships to fight against men and not against the winds and waves of God.'

Only a hundred years later, in 1688, we *were* invaded, very successfully, by a Dutchman. Lord Cameron of Chipping Norton's top childhood book, H. E. Marshall's *Our Island Story*, offers this by way of summary: 'The people were weary of a Popish tyrant, and they made up their minds to have a Protestant king.' This analysis has rather stuck, and you could argue it's true, but only if by *the people* you mean the aristocrats, and if by *Popish tyranny* you mean James II wanted Catholics to be allowed to worship in public. In fact it was, once again, about babies. The king's eldest daughter, Mary, was married to William, stadtholder of the United Provinces and a leading light of

Protestant Europe. Mary, whose brothers had all died in infancy, was heir to the throne, and the Protestant nobility reckoned they could cope with a Catholic king until James II's death and her accession. But then the king's second wife, who had lost *five* children, as well as suffering multiple miscarriages and stillbirths, gave birth to a son, James. He would, if he survived, be raised a Catholic and inherit the throne, which was beyond the Protestant pale. William and Mary were told the throne was theirs for the taking.

William was well prepared, and the Dutch were good seamen. His 50-strong fleet, plus 225 troop transports, put to sea in October, unaware that the forecast was GERMAN BIGHT, HUMBER, THAMES, south to southwest 5 to 6, veering west 7 or gale force 8 later. That *later* really did for them. The invasion force was scattered, but it managed to regroup at Hellevoetsluis, with the only casualties being 400 horses who'd suffocated below decks when their grooms were too seasick to look after them. The Dutch news sheets over-egged the damage, and James, who'd had an enormous weathercock mounted on the roof of the Banqueting House opposite his Whitehall apartments, thought a 'Popish wind' had answered his prayers.

But all too soon the wind turned Protestant once more, and the Dutch fleet gave the (frankly hopeless) British fleet the slip, sailing gaily down-Channel, pennants streaming, guns trumpeting, sails glittering, music thrumming, lights sparkling, landing at Torbay unopposed. This William, says Cameron's history primer, was no conqueror, but a *deliverer*, which might have made sense to English Protestants, but certainly didn't to the Irish, Scottish and English Catholics, who plotted and fought to restore first the king, then his son, then his grandson (a.k.a. Bonnie Prince Charlie) to the throne. But despite nearly six decades of conflict, the fall of James II has somehow always been painted as a very best-of-British sort of revolution: modest, genial, bloodless, quite different from the American and French revolutions which followed.

Napoleon Bonaparte, who took up the reins of Revolutionary France in 1799, was the next man to have serious designs on the White Cliffs. He upped the ante, promising to abolish the monarchy and the House of Lords, and found a republic based on liberty, equality and fraternity, with the small caveat that he was well on his way to becoming an emperor, ermine robes and all.

After previous attempts to invade via Ireland or Wales had backfired, Napoleon decided to focus on the direct route, mustering his 167,000-strong Army of England at Boulogne, where he made preparations to leap the 'ditch'. 'Let us,' he said, 'be masters of the Channel for six hours and we are masters of the world.' To which

Admiral Lord St Vincent (is said to have) replied: 'I do not say the French cannot come – I only say they cannot come by sea.' Napoleon's troop transports were primarily oar-powered, so what he needed was THAMES DOVER WIGHT, variable 0 to 3, fair, moderate with occasional fog patches, allowing him to speed across the Channel, while the Royal Navy's ships flogged and flapped, harmless as beached whales. From his station blockading the French port of Toulon, Vice-Admiral Horatio Nelson was to taunt him for what turned into months of delay: 'He begins to find excuses!' he wrote to a friend. 'I thought he would invade England in the face of the Sun! Now he wants a three-days' fog that never yet happened!'

Since the 1790s, when it first became clear that one way or another France meant to invade, Britain had been gripped by waves of rabid speculation. Napoleon would arrive in a hot-air balloon! Through a tunnel! Across a bridge built right across the Channel! He was going to rename London Bonapartopolis! Damn and blast it all, John Bull would be set to hoeing vasty fields of garlic! Even the Romantic poets, who were normally very keen on liberty etc., got a bit misty-eyed. A callow Samuel Taylor Coleridge enlisted as a private under the pseudonym Silas Tomkyn Comberbache; his big brothers paid a bribe to bail him out. William Wordsworth, too, thumped the patriotic tub hard: 'Ye men of Kent, 'tis victory or death!' (which was easy to say when you lived in Grasmere).

Happily for the nation (if not for this chapter), the invasion turned out to be a damp squib. The Austrians declared war on Napoleon, and he headed east, trouncing them at the Battle of Austerlitz in 1805, while the decisive naval engagement of the Napoleonic Wars was fought not in DOVER, but in TRAFALGAR, which is a great story, but one which doesn't belong here.

And now, the moment we've all been waiting for, the two crucial crossings of the Second World War: the evacuation of Dunkirk in 1940 and the D-Day landings in 1944. Don't be tempted to think that because we'd ditched sail, the weather didn't matter. In both cases, the West Wind's backing was as decisive for Winston Churchill as it had been for Elizabeth I.

Dunkirk first. The British Expeditionary Force, outnumbered and outfought, was retreating before the Nazi advance; the Nazis held Calais and Boulogne, so the only feasible place from which the British could escape back home was Dunkirk. The city was a smoking ruin. The sea was slick with oil, dotted with stricken vessels and drowned bodies. The beaches were littered with abandoned kit – and orderly lines of men. Cue Operation Dynamo, which saw the navy requisitioning small fishing and pleasure boats

(many of which had been mothballed since the start of the war) to cross the Channel in convoy to ferry soldiers off the beaches and onto bigger ships waiting offshore.

The *London Gazette*, the government's in-house newspaper, wrote: 'It must be fully realised that a wind of any strength in the northern sector between South West and North East would have made beach evacuation impossible.' Why? Breakers. It's *extremely* difficult to land or launch boats in surf. As we know, westerly winds, strong or otherwise, are the Channel's buttered bread but, as it turned out, we got incredibly lucky. Sure, it was early summer, but as anyone who's spent May half-term crabbing with toddlers in the pissing rain can attest, that's no guarantee of anything. As it was, from 26 May to 4 June, the weather was remarkably benign, and Operation Dynamo was able to rescue 340,000 soldiers, seven or eight times as many the navy's most optimistic original estimate. The *Shipping Forecast* for DOVER on 26 May this year? Southwest 4 to 6. Same on 27 May. We'd have been *stuffed*.

Now for D-Day, which was essentially Dunkirk, but in reverse. For the Allies to greenlight the largest amphibious assault in history, to end the Nazi occupation of Europe, they had to wait on what the Met Office calls 'the most important weather forecast in history'; fighting talk, but I think we can allow it.

A Royal Navy meteorologist, the New Zealand-born Lawrence Hogben, said the D-Day planners told the forecasting team to name five fine, calm days. Can you hear the laughter echoing down the decades? 'A hundred years of weather records suggested there was no hope of their getting this,' Hogben wrote in a fascinating account, published by the *London Review of Books* in 1994. The top brass trimmed their shopping list to 'a quiet day with not more than moderate winds and seas and not too much cloud for the airmen, to be followed by three more quiet days', which is like saying if you can't get me a star, I'll settle for the moon. And it couldn't be any old quiet day: the commanders wanted a full moon, with a tide that was low but rising at dawn, all of which created huge pressure to make 5 or 6 June work.

On 4 June, observations from ships far out in the Atlantic reported a low south of Iceland, which would move across the north of Britain. The brash know-nothing American forecasters weren't worried. 'Fuggedaboutit! Don't listen to those yellow-bellied limeys. We're good to go!' But the buttoned-up Brits knew best. Group Captain James Stagg had the unenviable task of persuading Dwight 'Ike' Eisenhower, the Supreme Allied Commander, that D-Day could not possibly happen on 5 June. In the teeth of intense pressure, he stuck to his guns. Come the early hours, as he predicted (and doubtless to his immense relief), the low was hammering Britain, bringing with it strong winds, heavy rain and appalling visibility, all of which would have combined to scupper the landings.*

But while everyone else was cursing our rotten luck, Stagg was still poring over his synoptic charts, and it was then that he spotted something – a gap. He saw that that next depression in the West Wind's rack, still off the coast of Newfoundland, was slowing down. There was, his meteorological antennae told him, the tiniest window of opportunity. Not a fine, calm day, no, but a breather, a respite, a chance for the wind and waves to moderate enough, *just* enough, to make the landings possible. The Germans, clueless without this vital mid-Atlantic weather data, assumed the terrible weather on 5 June would rule out 6 June as well. They poured a libation to the West Wind and relaxed. The West Wind smirked, and there, *there*, was a little ridge of high pressure, right where Stagg said it would be. The D-Day landings were a success, and the rest, as they say, is history.

It was a truly amazing call.

*

---

* There was similarly vile weather on 5 June 2022, Elizabeth II's Jubilee weekend. A vicious squall-line marched right through our village tug-o'-war.

Up until now, we've been thinking about when *we* were under threat. But, of course, for the last half a millennium, streams of English and British ships have been crossing the other way. All too often, the Channel, far from being a barricade, has acted as a runway, a launchpad. The *Heart of Darkness* narrator calls the Thames 'the beginning of an interminable waterway'; 'a waterway leading to the uttermost ends of the earth'; 'that river into the mystery of the unknown earth'; an earth which we, indubitably, have exploited.

Our triumph over the Spanish Armada, our increasing naval prowess and maritime dominance, gave us the confidence to challenge Spain and Portugal on their own turf: the acquisition of colonies and the trafficking of enslaved people to work in those colonies.* 'English involvement in the slave trade,' explains Michael Taylor in *The Interest*, his account of how the establishment, including peers, civil servants, businessmen, financiers, landowners, clergymen,

---

* Back when Charles Darwin was with Robert FitzRoy on the *Beagle*, one of the biggest rows they had was about enslaved people. Darwin wrote: 'We had several quarrels, for when out of temper he was utterly unreasonable. For instance, early in the voyage at Bahia in Brazil he defended and praised the slavery which I abominated, and told me that he had just visited a great slave owner, who had called up many of his slaves and asked them whether they were happy, and whether they wished to be free, and all answered no. I then asked him perhaps with a sneer, whether he thought that the answer of slaves in the presence of their master was worth anything. This made him excessively angry, and he said that as I doubted his word we could not live any longer together.' (They subsequently made up.)

intellectuals, journalists, publishers, sailors, soldiers and judges defended the indefensible in the name of profit, 'began as a simple matter of jealousy.' Our southern rivals were raking it in, and 'the English had a basic, piratical desire to share in the spoils'.

Popular historiography, though, has preferred to jump as nimbly as possible from the Armada heroes' first slaving ventures, to an acknowledgment of the horrific conditions on the Middle Passage and in the colonies, to arrive happily at the passionate abolition campaign of William Wilberforce and friends, which culminated in the Slave Trade Act in 1807, the first tiny step in ending centuries of abuse. The brain is a hero-maker, and it has always been comforting to tell ourselves nice stories about nice abolitionists and nasty plantation owners, about nice navy ships hunting down nasty slavers, rather than to confront the truth, which was that British society profited at almost every level. And yet, as the Caribbean historian and statesman Eric Williams drily observed in *British Historians and the West Indies*, 'The British historians wrote almost as if Britain had introduced Negro slavery solely for the satisfaction of abolishing it'.

I can be as much of a patriotic sap as the next person. When, in Christopher Nolan's *Dunkirk*, an exhausted Kenneth Branagh, pallid as his iconic roll-neck, spots the first hazy dots on the calm Channel, when an aide hands him binoculars and asks, 'What do you see?', when Branagh hesitates, replies, '*Home*,' when the music changes from weird and edgy and discordant to the rousing strings of what can only be a spin on Elgar's 'Nimrod', I well right up.* Some of us do undoubtedly owe our lives to those small boats – but many more of us are here today because our ancestors were taken in English/British ships to English/British colonies to work on English/British plantations. Tom Nancollas, whose *The Ship Asunder* is a brilliant celebration of Britain's maritime history, writes: 'We are beginning to look at our seafaring heritage with clearer eyes: now the challenge is to let no part of it, whether good or bad, ever sink again.'

Where are we today? You can staycation in Martello towers built to defend us from Napoleon. You can hire Victorian naval forts in WIGHT for epic parties. You can eat peanut-butter sandwiches on the steps of Second World War bunkers on Steep Holm in the Bristol Channel. There's the odd fillip of excitement when a whale braves the shipping lanes, but otherwise nothing prowls off DOVER. And yet we are, according to some, still very much under threat.

---

* I also cried when I saw the spot on HMS *Victory* where Nelson died in Captain Hardy's arms, which some might say is going a *bit* far.

Migrants and/or refugees pay smugglers thousands of pounds for the privilege of attempting to cross the Channel in overcrowded, unseaworthy boats, leading to nearly a hundred people drowning in the past six years, including a seven-year-old girl. The situation, according to the *Economist*, has evolved from a 'curiosity' to a 'political nightmare'. It was easy to turn a blind eye back when only a few hundred people made the crossing every year, but after 46,000 people landed in 2022, with another 30,000 in 2023, it has become impossible to look away. I don't know the answer to this problem, nor do I envy the politicians, civil servants and enforcement officers who urgently need to find one. But I do know that when we hear the *Shipping Forecast* pass through DOVER, we should ask the West Wind to show mercy to those who are about to risk their lives on one of the most unpredictable stretches of water in the world. 'This is seafaring,' writes Nancollas with exemplary empathy, 'stripped back to its basics, by people who don't want to be seafarers at all.'

TIDELINE

Your title, thence, sir,
Duke of the Drowned-lands

Ben Jonson, *The Devil Is an Ass* (1616)

Let's enjoy a lull after all that cannon fire. Let's sit beside the kindly Mrs Ramsay, a portrait of Virginia Woolf's mother, who'd died suddenly when she was thirteen, a woman whom her sister, Vanessa Bell, said lived and breathed again at the heart of *To the Lighthouse*, the writer's most popular and (for our purposes) most maritime novel. It was published when the *Shipping Forecast* was three years old, and I like to imagine Woolf pausing over her proofs, pencil raised, catching fragments of sound from a neighbouring room, hearing *fair, good*, and smiling to herself, thinking, yes, that's it, that's her, that's what she was like.

The book, set in an imagined HEBRIDES, rather than the St Ives of her real and really happy childhood holidays, starts with a tussle over a weather forecast. Mrs Ramsay's small son longs to visit the lighthouse the next day, but her husband pours cold water on the idea: 'Not with the barometer falling and the wind due west.' A little later, soothing her son and his dashed hopes, Mrs Ramsay is struck by the sound of the waves, which she normally finds soothing, 'some old cradle song, murmured by nature', but now, quite suddenly, they make her think 'of the destruction of the island and its engulfment in the sea'.

That reverie – of destruction, of engulfment – is especially hard to read, knowing what we know about how Woolf chose to end her life, walking into the River Ouse with her pockets full of stones. But thoughts of destruction, thoughts of engulfment have long been the spectral phosphorescence in humanity's wake. The world's oldest written story, *He Who Saw the Deep*, a surprisingly readable* 4,000-year-old Mesopotamian epic about our fear of death, includes an account of its hero, Gilgamesh, visiting Utnapishtim, a legendary king whose boat-building skills helped him and his family survive a deluge, sent by the gods, which swallowed up the rest of humankind. The critic Marina Warner (who compares the Akkadian script in which the poem is written to the prints of wading birds on ebb-tide sand) reminds us that, 'Myths, like inquisitive children, keep asking: why?' Why are we – culturally – so obsessed with flood stories?

---

* Readability evidencing line: 'The ocean, which had thrashed like a woman in labour, grew calm.'

Here in Britain, we're used to how every day, four times a day (or, to be precise, every 6 hours, 12 minutes and 30 seconds) the sea advances and retreats, advances and retreats, remaking the land before our eyes. But for nearly a thousand generations, the waters have really only been going in one direction: *up*.

Year after year, I've been watching the slow dissolution of an out-of-the-way patch of PLYMOUTH coast. When I was young, two concrete jetties, connected by a chunk of sea-wall, framed a little beach, backed up by rows of wooden groynes, their upright posts sunk into concrete. As I graduated from building sandcastles, to rock-hurling battles, to drinking cider, to helping my children with their own castles, the jetties have cracked, the wall has slumped, the groynes have been washed away. Every winter, more sand, more land, is gouged away. Later this century, one grey dawn when a force 10 storm meets a full-moon high tide, the house where we holiday, fifty flat yards inshore, will flood. (I have a recurring dream of the sea sluicing through the marram grass, along the bracken path, pouring under the gate.) Later this millennium, the house, like countless others, will be gone.

Global ice cover reached a peak maybe 20–26,000 years ago – the Last Glacial Maximum – after which, in fits and starts, it began to retreat. That retreat, that mass melt, had nothing to do with us. Instead, it was triggered by tilts and wobbles in the Earth's orbit and axis, tweaks on a celestial dimmer switch, which increased the amount of sunlight hitting the planet.* The upshot? Since the end of the last ice age, global sea levels have risen by as much as 120 metres, meaning across cultures and continents, from the Jewish Torah to the Hindu Mahābhārata to the Aboriginal Dreaming, we meet story after story, some confirmed by paleoarchaeology, of how cities, valleys, islands, entire peoples have drowned.

Here in Britain, the impact of sea-level rise has fallen – and will fall – more on our southern and eastern coasts. That same line which divided Rome from not-Rome, not-Celt from Celt, is also a rough guide to our geology, and hence to our vulnerability. The north and west of Britain is, by and large, made up of higher ground and harder rocks, the upland regurgitations of volcanoes. The south and east, on average, is made up of younger, softer, crumblier rocks, the lowland strata of silts and shells. To double down, the north of Britain was, for millennia, squashed under a mile-thick layer of ice. Now ice-less,

---

* Climate-change deniers have jumped on the past to minimise the present: no no no, they say, *natural variations*, that's all, nothing to see here, nothing we can do. In fact, even if natural variations got global warming started, we have floored the accelerator.

it has been infinitesimally rebounding. We are living on a seesaw. Top going up. Bottom going down. The line between land and sea is wavering. The *Shipping Forecast*'s stomping ground is growing.

Back when the ice finally quit our corner of the Atlantic, only Ireland was an island. Britain was still a promontory, connected to the continent by a boggy soggy landmass, which now lies doggo beneath the North Sea. For decades, mysterious bones found their way into the nets of boats fishing the DOGGER bank, evidence of a world – christened Doggerland – lost beneath the waves. Ed Conway, whose *Material World* is an exploration of some of the natural resources we take for granted, relates a surprising collision of past and present. London's concrete, he explains, has a mystical backstory: much of it is made from sand and aggregate scraped from the Doggerland seabed, using machines which have been known to clog with mammoth tusks, rhino teeth and human hand-axes. 'Next time,' he says, 'you see a concrete block in Britain's capital and are tempted to dismiss it as a modernist monstrosity, ponder for a moment that it may well have been made of the sands from this mysterious drowned world, out in the middle of the North Sea.'

But Doggerland is far from unique. All around Britain, the shoreline would once have stretched miles further than it does today. A mesolithic child, gobbling up whortleberries on the northern flank of the Quantock Hills, wouldn't have seen Steep Holm as an island in the Bristol Channel, but as a hillock in a marshy plain. St Michael's Mount, a tidal island on Cornwall's south coast, used to stand proud in a sea of trees, a past preserved in its Cornish name, Karrek Loos yn Koos: the grey rock in the wood. The Solent, too, was a river valley, and where fibreglass yachts, RIBs and jet-skis now zig and zag, aurochs and woolly mammoths did solemnly graze.

More remarkably still, until perhaps 12,000 years ago, the Isles of Scilly were joined to the Cornwall mainland, marking the southwestern tip of a long slab of granite (feel free to call it the Cornubian batholith) which runs up to Dartmoor. Rising seas created one large Scilly Isle, before dicing it into smaller and smaller pieces, forcing islanders to retreat as tracts of land first became inter-tidal and then vanished altogether. Remnants of abandoned settlements, dry-stone walls and field boundaries are still exposed at low water today.

Over the centuries, then, Cornish folklore and Arthurian legend have collaborated to give us the myth of Lyonesse, a lost land which lies between the mainland

and the Scillies, of which the granite peaks of the Seven Stones Reef, barely awash at high water, might be the last vestigial sign. Sir Thomas Malory, in his fifteenth-century prose epic *Le Morte d'Arthur*, made Lyonesse the birthplace of Tristan, Knight of the Round Table, doomed lover of Isolde. Subsequent antiquarians, from the Enlightenment onwards, loved to write up tales of fishermen hooking doors and windows out of the depths, as well as sharing that perennial favourite, the sound of church bells echoing beneath the waves. Alfred, Lord Tennyson, Queen Victoria's favourite, also gave Lyonesse a boost, telling us in his *Idylls of the King* that Merlin himself drowned the 'land of old upheaven from the abyss' after King Arthur and his treacherous son Mordred fought their tragic showdown on its shores.

Contemporary artists have taken up the baton. In her second studio album, *Le Kov*, the Welsh–Cornish singer Gwenno Saunders invites us to join her between Land's End and the Scilly Rocks, to come to a sunken city, a bustling metropolis, a Cornish capital, a place of memory. The pysch-pop lyrics are sung entirely in Cornish, a language which itself came within a whisker of being swamped. When she sings it, she says, 'I can get lost, and everyone else has to get lost, because what else can they do?' But her songwriting wasn't only inspired by Lyonesse:

she looked to other legendary lands, including Cantre'r Gwaelod, which lies further north, in Wales, in Cardigan Bay. There are a slew of different stories about its demise, but one tells how it was protected from the sea by a dyke, with sluice gates that were closed at high tide. One night, though, a storm blew up from the southwest, driving the spring tide hard against the defences. The watchman, a heavy drinker, was partying and failed to shut the gates in time. The land drowned. Today, the woodlands of Cantre'r Gwaelod occasionally emerge at low tide, the petrified stumps swathed in ghostly robes of laver.

On Britain's east coast, though, vanished towns belong to history not myth. In its thirteenth-century heyday, Dunwich was a hub for merchants from across the *Shipping Forecast* map, north to the UTSIREs, south to BISCAY. Its population was a sixth the size of London's, and with its churches and convents, its shipyards and fortifications, I'd wager it would have outshone Lyonesse itself. And now? Population 120, one pub, not even a Co-op. W.G. Sebald (or at least his fictional alter ego) visited what's left of Dunwich at the end of the last century, finding it preternaturally suited to his preoccupation with loss and decay. 'He' tells us how on New Year's Eve 1285, a storm hit, causing so much devastation that 'for months afterwards no one could tell where the land ended and the sea began'. Forty years later, the seas returned. 'As darkness fell, those living around the harbour fled with whatever belongings they could carry to the upper town. All night the waves clawed away one row of houses after another.' That absence moved him profoundly. 'If you look out from the cliff-top across the sea towards where the town must once have been, you can sense the immense power of emptiness.'*

Destruction on that scale exists well within living memory: the North Sea flood of 1953 killed 307 people. On the night between 31 January and 1 February, a big spring tide and a deep Atlantic depression combined to send a wall of water down the east coast, drowning men, women and children in their beds. In Hilda Grieve's *The Great Tide*, a social history as moving as it is detailed, we read how, with little or no warning, the horrific storm-surge overwhelmed our sea defences, devastating major towns and tiny villages.

Canvey Island, much of which lies below the THAMES estuary high-water level at the best of times, was especially badly hit. People were woken by a roar as the island's sea-wall burst, sending waves and debris clattering, crashing

---

* On a lighter note, my fellow daughters and sons of the 1980s may recall Baldrick's questionable victory at the Dunny-on-the-Wold by-election in *Blackadder the Third*. Until the 1832 Great Reform Act, Dunwich was indeed the rottenest of rotten boroughs, sending a pair of MPs to Westminster despite being more or less under water.

and swirling round their houses. Often their only chance of survival lay in punching through their flimsy ceilings into the roof-space above, or in hauling themselves up onto their roofs. They clambered onto chairs, tables, cookers, mangle-tables and step-ladders, trying to keep their heads above water. Sometimes, wrote Grieve, their props were swept away from under them, leaving them 'fighting in the dark with floating furniture, clutching desperately at fanlights and the tops of doors and wardrobes, and trying to hold children up above the suffocating water'. In one bunga-low, there lived a family with nine children under 16. The father, standing on the table, lifted one after another into the roof space, until seven were safe. After that, the table disintegrated. The mother was left standing in water trying to hold up her two youngest boys. Both died in her arms.

Contemplating the sea's power, Daniel Defoe was inclined to throw up his hands in despair, musing in his *A Tour Thro' the Whole Island of Great Britain* that towns, like everything else, have 'their elevation, their medium, their declination, and even their destruction in the womb of time'. We rise, we fall, even as the tide. But those who live on vulnerable coastlines cannot afford to be so phlegmatic. With increasing skill and determination, we've learnt how to (try to) defend ourselves. 'Over the years,' writes Michael

Pye in *The Edge of the World*, 'even the coastline was fixed in place as it never used to be when high winds could make a storm out of the sand, and high tides could break deep into the land.' With embankments and esplanades, with groynes and gabions, with revetments and rip-rap, we've created what he calls 'a definite squared-off boundary between man and sea'.

The Thames Barrier, half a kilometre across, is our flagship defence. Conceived in the wake of the 1953 catastrophe, operational since 1982, its gates can be closed to stop storm surges barrelling upriver and flooding the capital. And yet, based on current climate predictions, within a century we're going to need a better barrier, and the same goes for many coastal defences around our shores. Instead of building walls high enough to withstand a 1-in-200-year flood scenario, we might need to start aping the Dutch, who designed the Maeslantkering, the barrier which protects the Port of Rotterdam, to be ready for a 1-in-10,000-year storm.

The Netherlands, after all, is much more vulnerable to sea-level rise, with a quarter of its land, in an already crowded country, well below sea level. Their tactic is to expect the worst, and to prep hard for it. They've had practice. Two thousand years ago, the Roman naturalist Pliny the Elder was already impressed with their building nous, describing how families lived in huts perched on man-made hummocks of high ground. They looked, he wrote, like sailors when floods covered the surrounding land.

It's easy to scare ourselves. We can open our laptops and peer into the future, toggling dates, climate scenarios, temperature increases, redrawing the coastline, wiping out tracts of southern and eastern England with one drag of our index fingers, sending villages, towns, counties tumbling into the sea. And yet, whatever we do, sea levels will continue to rise. How far and how fast depends on how far and how fast we cut greenhouse-gas emissions – and whether the rising temperatures we've already guaranteed ourselves trigger feedback loops, accelerating the pace of change. That could mean anything between a 0.5 and a 4.3 metre rise for the THAMES between now and 2300. By then, says the Met Office, what we'd think of today as a 1-in-10,000-year scenario could be an annual event.

Facing these sorts of threats, climate activists say, 'Let's turn this ship around.' After all, we're all in the same boat. Or are we? When the *Titanic* sailed from WIGHT in 1912, its lifeboats could only hold 1,178 people, a little over half of those on board that night. The subsequent inquiry revealed the ship's owners, the White Star Line, had (perfectly legally) trimmed the number of lifeboats to gussy up the ship's looks and to improve the first-class passengers' view. In Britain, there's a temptation to console ourselves that, in *Titanic* terms, we're fancy ladies sitting pretty in first class: 97 per cent of them made it, compared with 8 per cent of men in second. As a country, are we hoping to pull on our fur coats, grab our pearl necklaces, jump the lifeboat queue, and survive?

That's the approach Britain opts for in John Lanchester's *The Wall*, a dystopian view of our near-future. Faced with four degrees of warming, we've built a 10,000-kilometre 'long low concrete monster' around our coast to defend ourselves from refugees – known simply as the Others – fleeing the uninhabitable latitudes further south. The 'olds', perhaps those who are children now, can still remember beaches, ice-creams, surfing, fun. The young, meanwhile, are conscripted, forced to stand a two-year stint on the Wall. If an Other breaches their section while they're on watch, they're set adrift in a small boat – banished from Britain.

In *Flood*, a novel by hard sci-fi pro Stephen Baxter, the whole of humanity winds up at sea. It takes about 30 years (let's not worry overmuch about the mechanism) for the waters to rise 8,800 metres, slower than the biblical 40 days and 40 nights, but fast enough that by the time Everest sinks beneath the waves, a few old-timers are still whanging on about reading and writing, about latitude

and longitude, about civilisation.* Watching the children
of the future happily catching fish with their teeth, sucking
their eyeballs for water, watching young mothers giving
birth in the sea, some of them are aghast. 'We can't,' one
guy exclaims, 'let our kids turn into fucking seals.' But
others are impressed by the next generation's ease, their
adaptability, their grace. See, they say, whatever you throw
at it, humanity will find a way to survive. Let's hope we do.

We are caught in a vice of cognitive dissonance: two
very different things are true at once. We watch the sea
scouring the land, and know we are ultimately powerless
to stop it, while at the same time knowing that it is, in part,
our fault. We are powerful; we are powerless. The tideline is littered with the wrack of nature, with seaweed and
sandhoppers, with mermaids' purses and cuttlebones, but
it is also strewn with flip-flops and bottle-tops – with the
detritus of civilisation.

From the gods' POV, our hopes and fears, our sea-wall
upgrades and shoreline management plans, our electric
cars and our ground-sourced heat pumps, might very well
look as sweet and pointless as children frantically filling
buckets, trying to save their castles from the tide. Heap the
sand higher and higher. Add more stones. Dig a channel,

* Before things got really serious, I was pleased to find my hometown
re-imagined as a tanker port, a rare fictional name-check for Taunton.

divert the water. Quick, quick, build another one further up the beach. When the children admit defeat, they get an ice cream. They get to come back to the beach the next day. They get to start all over again. What about us? What can we do?

Witness the famous bait and switch at the denouement of the original 1968 *Planet of the Apes*. A man and a woman are riding a horse along a beautiful beach. She is a local, an escapee from the ape overlords. He is a spaceman, who crash-landed in this alien world. But no – what's that? In the bottom left-hand corner of the screen, something moves into view. It's too close. The camera can't make sense of what it sees. The angle shifts. Iconic head spikes fill the screen. The man leaps off his horse. Waves sluice around his bare legs. He's recognised the Statue of Liberty. The planet is our own. He falls to his knees, cursing humanity for having destroyed the world. The waves do what waves do: they wash over him. Deep down, we know that every-thing – our lives, the *Shipping Forecast*, Britain itself – is, as Mrs Ramsay says to herself, 'all ephemeral as a rainbow'.

BOOTY

he liked men to work like that, and women to keep house, and sit beside sleeping children indoors, while men were drowned, out there in a storm

Virginia Woolf, *To the Lighthouse* (1927)

IN MY EARLY TWENTIES, I was staying at one of the many B&Bs near the HUMBER waterfront at Cleethorpes, Grimsby's upmarket neighbour. I was doing a couple of weeks' work experience at the *Grimsby Telegraph*, which I'd heard (at a time when the local-journalism ebb was well underway) was a brilliant newspaper. I had a tiny room, a shared bathroom, and ate powdered eggs and soggy toast for breakfast. I was tucking up after a night out in the pub with colleagues (who mocked me gently for my southern coat-wearing ways), when there was a riotous hammering on my bedroom door, followed by a riotous medley of male voices. They were non-trivially drunk, but their gist wasn't hard to catch.

Little girl, little girl, can we come in?

Not by the hair on my chinny-chin-chin.

They huffed and puffed, really quite a lot, but they didn't quite blow my door in.

The next morning, when I made my way gingerly downstairs for breakfast, the owner apologised sheepishly. He said they'd meant no harm. He said they were back from offshore (I didn't ask what doing; some journalist, me), they were off home that day, and I wasn't to worry.

Later that week, I was beckoned into the editor's office. He said he was going to offer me a proper job, which he knew I wouldn't take, because he knew, more fool me, that I had delusions of London grandeur. We chatted for a while, and he told me a bit about Grimsby's history that I'd been too lackadaisical to find out for myself before I got on the train north. He told me it used to be the fishing capital of the world. He told me about the wives of fishermen walking to meet their husbands at the docks, decked out in furs and jewels. He told me about the pubs, heaving with men, flush with fish cash, high on dry land, desperate to spend spend spend after weeks at sea. He made a very great impression on me as a smart and decent man who cared deeply about his town and his job, a man who believed in his power to make a difference. But I couldn't marry up the picture he'd painted with the down-on-its-luck place where I'd been working.

We have become increasingly divorced from the business of the sea, which used to be such a big feature of so many of our towns and cities, from the capital itself to the dozens and dozens of cargo and fishing ports that ringed the country round. In *Redburn*, Herman Melville's semi-autobiographical account of a callow youth's adventures in nineteenth-century Liverpool, he emphasises his hero's sense of awe and wonder, comparing the port to the Great Wall of China – to the Great Lakes – to the pyramids of Egypt. Each dock, he says, 'is a walled town, full of life and commotion; or rather, it is a small archipelago, an epitome of the world'. Nowadays, 95 per cent of our imports and exports still travel by sea, but the graft happens out of sight, out of mind, in a small number of intensely busy, purpose-built container ports. Small harbours have been revamped to appeal to day-trippers after a dose of salt, vinegar and seaweed. City docks have been scrubbed down, decked out with salvaged anchors, and packed full of chain restaurants, Laser Quest and two-bed apartments. The business, the *work*, happens elsewhere.

My nearest harbour is Watchet in LUNDY, twenty minutes' drive away. I love it. I love the statue of the Ancient Mariner and his albatross. I love the tubby yachts sinking into the Somerset mud. I love the two – two!!! – museums, the cool new gallery, the old-school tea-room, the secondhand shops, the ice-cream parlour. To me, it's perfect in every way. But really not so very long ago, well into the twentieth century, it was a serious import–export harbour, landing coal, wine and brandy, legit or otherwise, and dispatching lime (including for the Eddystone Lighthouse), iron (from the Brendon Hills), paper (from the Wansbrough Paper Mill, which only closed a decade ago), as well as seaweed, alabaster, gypsum, wool, and of course fish. It wasn't until 1999 that it officially retired as a commercial harbour.

That's the world the Grimsby newspaper editor had been trying to tell me about, a world where the maritime economy was the heart and soul of a place, where the work was alive, kicking and able to give people a strong sense of identity, of belonging – a world where the *Shipping Forecast* was prose not poetry. But if, as happened in Grimsby, the work dried up suddenly, if the core industry tanked, the knock-on effect – on the fishermen, on the industries that supported them – was rough.

'It was a good life, fishing,' Earnest 'Dutchy' Holland told the authors of *Fish 'n' Ships* (a chef's kiss of a title), an own-voices retrospective of the Grimsby fishing industry. At its peak, Grimsby was a boom town. The Klondyke of the East. A local fishocracy grew rich. The town bustled. Businesses, the ice factory, the chandlers, the pubs, the taxis, they all thrived. The Grimsby Dock Tower, a beautiful slipcase for some meaty Victorian hydraulics, modelled on a medieval original in Siena, was a totem of civic self-confidence.

Continues Holland: 'Everybody that came from Grimsby, no matter what you were on the ship, you had a pride that, you know, you was a Grimsby fisherman.'

Of course, it wasn't always pretty. Back in the nineteenth century, hapless boys were lured to sea, signing their lives away as apprentices. If they tried to quit, they'd be done for desertion under the 1854 Merchant Shipping Act and banged up. In a scene that belongs in Charles Dickens's still-undiscovered fishing novel, one Alderman Mudd [*sic*] apparently toasted the local magistrates for keeping the labour force of seasick, terrorised teenagers on the straight and narrow. To make up for their hard life – there are reports of farmers' sons yanked overboard and drowned the first time they tried to fill a bucket from the deck of a boat that was underway – the 'fisherlads', much to the chagrin of hand-wringing moralists, made a beeline for the town's brothels, pubs and music halls, rather than taking up the hearty sports the philanthropists arranged for them. The fishermen themselves were diddled by the men who actually owned the fleet, finding themselves facing huge bills for ice, food and coal that ate into the money they made from their catch. And the job didn't become any easier in the twentieth century.

Remember the icing we met in WEATHER? Another Grimsby fisherman, Dave Pratt, explained that in the winter a half-inch wire could turn four inches thick with ice inside an hour: 'Then we call the watches out, get the axes out and start chopping away. Too much top ice will turn the ship over.' The whole crew would be hacking away, eyelashes and nose-hairs freezing solid, frantic, frightened – but not letting on. Sometimes, conditions were so bad, the waves so big, that a man might be swept overboard. The lucky ones managed to cling on, or were grabbed by a mate, or found the next wave washed them back aboard. Nevertheless, the stats are terrifying. Between 1961 and 1980, one fisherman died on average every eight days at sea, and that's not counting those who died of injuries later on shore. The trauma, you can be sure, was processed by the tried-and-tested formula of a lot of drinking and not much talking. The wife of one man who fell overboard says her husband never let on what happened: 'It was one of his mates that told me about two trips later. He wouldn't tell me.'

So, a hard job – but oh, the joy of return. The boats came steaming back up HUMBER, the fishermen in their best gear, knowing wives, children, girlfriends would be waiting as they entered the lock gates. They were kings for the day, in their glad-rags, trying to cram the weeks they missed at sea into a few days on shore. Fishermen acquired a reputation.* Mothers told their daughters not to bring one into the house. Drink. Women. Drink. Women. But there are other, quieter stories too: like the man who quit fishing because his son couldn't sleep at night for fear of his dad dying.

And now? The fishermen in *Fish 'n' Ships* take up the story: 'It's absolutely dead, it's just like going down a graveyard.'

'A ghost town.'

What banjaxed the fishing industry? First, overfishing in home waters. Second, quotas in European waters: once we joined the EEC in 1973, we had to share. Third, geopolitics. If we wanted more fish, we had to go further afield, especially to the seas around Iceland. But the Icelanders needed those fish even more than we did, and fought hard – both metaphorically around the negotiating table and literally out at sea – to keep them. (Think ramming

---

* In the early twentieth century, one group of women had the chance to acquire a reputation of their own. Every summer, thousands of 'herring lasses' left Scottish fishing towns and villages and followed the boats working their way down the east coast. Their job was to gut the annual herring bonanza, sorting and prepping the catch, packing millions upon millions of fish into salting barrels. They travelled, lived, worked – and played – independently, prompting the genteel townsfolk down south to brand them rough, coarse, even immoral. But for the women themselves, the reward for weeks of hard and dirty work was camaraderie, adventure and the novelty of dance halls, cinemas and department stores. It also changed their view of their lives back home. Writes Donald S. Murray in *Herring Tales*, 'No longer would women settle for what they had put up with for centuries.'

and net-cutting not ballistics.) The Cod Wars, as they became known, coincided with the Cold War, and Iceland discovered that its proximity to the Soviet Union was an ace up its sleeve. If the UK tried to stop them claiming sole access to all the cod within an ever-expanding radius of their coast, they'd be far less co-operative about NATO deploying kit on their highly strategic territory. The US leant on the UK, we backed down – and our defeat in the Cod Wars is seen as a national humiliation to this day.

But the collapse of the offshore fishing industry was about more than economics: it was also a serious blow to male pride. The novelist and journalist James Meek, who visited Grimsby in the run-up to the Brexit vote, compared fishermen and coalminers: 'two groups of skilled work-ers winning goods from nature, exploited and well paid at the same time, doing hard jobs that women didn't do, for whom the danger was not only a source of menace but also of pride, a way to test your manhood in front of other men.' The town's long-serving Labour MP, Austin Mitchell, who was so committed to his adopted town that he once changed his name by deed poll to Austin Haddock,* was especially impressed by this sort of toughness. He looked back on the commanding heights of the fishing industry

---

* This is, undoubtably, the place to mention that Captain Haddock's name was suggested to Hergé by his wife as an archetypal 'sad English fish'.

as a time when 'men were men', and he was certainly far from alone in being intoxicated by the potency of fish. A veteran local Labour campaigner told Meek that Mitchell's predecessor in parliament, an intellectual middle-class southerner called Anthony Crosland, also over-idealised the town's machismo: "'He liked the working class," she said. "I think he was just in love with the concept. I think if he'd seen the women being beaten up when the lads came home from the sea he'd have had a different viewpoint.'"

Just as fish were shrinking into the shadows, another (even more?) macho commodity stepped into the limelight: oil. If you go north from HUMBER, past the defunct steel, coal and shipbuilding industries on TYNE and FORTH, you arrive at CROMARTY and Aberdeen, the hub of Britain's – or Scotland's, depending on your POV – oil industry. Back in the sixties, just like Grimsby, the city ran on fish. Ian Jack, journalist and author of *Before the Oil Ran Out*, remembers holidaying in the Silver* City with the Golden Sands when he was a boy: 'We ate boiled and fried haddock for a week and were reminded constantly that Aberdeen was then the premier fishing port of Europe.' The tourism

---

* The city's built from granite, which sparkles in the sun.

industry slumped after contaminated Argentinian corned-beef infected hundreds of people with typhoid, but soon Aberdeen wouldn't need fish or visitors. In 1969, prospectors working offshore struck oil.

Today, the Admiralty charts that cover VIKING and FORTIES are scribbled all over with the symbols for oil rigs and pipelines. Pass by at night, and the lonely sea and the sky are lit up like brutalist Christmas trees. An interviewee in a Radio 4 documentary described their gonzo visual impact perfectly: 'It was like seeing *The War of the Worlds* come striding across the water.'

But if the oil price hadn't rocketed in the early seventies, this radical transformation mightn't have happened at all. 'It was,' explains Mike Shepherd in *Oil Strike North Sea*, 'a Middle Eastern war that changed the North Sea forever.' In 1973, a coalition of Arab states invaded Israel; the US armed Israel; OPEC, the Saudi-dominated oil cartel, slapped a partial oil embargo on the West; the oil price quadrupled (and went higher still after the 1979 Iranian Revolution). Geopolitics, then, transformed attitudes towards the oil, buried as it was deep below a wild and stormy sea, from more-trouble-than-it's-worth to when-can-we-start? The government, unsurprisingly, was hungry for oil revenues. 'God,' said the Labour prime minister James Callaghan, in power 1976–9, 'has given

Britain her best opportunity for one hundred years in the shape of North Sea oil.' Certainly, at a time of soaring inflation, underinvestment and industrial unrest, when we had to go 'cap in hand' to the International Monetary Fund after the humiliating sterling crisis of 1976, we needed all the divine intervention we could get.*

We knew we had an amazing resource, but we didn't have the skills to tap it, so we drafted in US companies to sort us out. They drove a hard bargain, trying to browbeat us oil newbies into letting them pay as little tax as humanly possible. When we toughened up and introduced a raft of legislation, one Labour negotiator said Exxon wrote him a letter 'so rude that I could only assume it was drafted by someone accustomed to addressing banana republics'. Nevertheless, by the time the money began to roll in – and roll in it surely did – Labour was out of office. Margaret Thatcher won the 1979 election, and the Tories spent the next 18 years in power, with the tax receipts from our black gold flowing into the Treasury's coffers. We don't really think of ourselves as a petro-state, and yet for a chunk of the nineties, we were the ninth largest producer in the world.

---

* That IMF humiliation, for those of us who weren't politically conscious in 1976, was largely responsible for the lingering 'vibe' that Labour wasn't to be trusted on the economy; props to Liz 'Lettuce' Truss for putting things on a more even keel.

The oil rush, writes Jonathan Raban in *Coasting*, his account of cruising round Britain in the early eighties, turned Aberdeen into a mythical city: its 'amazing renaissance was talked of in places as far away even as London'. He'd heard the reports of swaggering Texas oilmen, all Stetsons and Chevies, and fantasised about soaking up some good vibes in this flashy oasis of prosperity. Frankly, he needed a narrative 'crock of gold', a happy ending to his otherwise downbeat voyage. Spoiler alert: he overshoots Aberdeen in thick fog, and winds up bobbing up and down in the city's sewage outfall.*

A decade later, the Scottish historian and politician Christopher Harvie was still waiting for a literary reckoning. 'Oil,' he wrote in *Fool's Gold*, 'failed almost totally to surface in the imaginative literature of Anglo-Britain.' But if we didn't get Jilly Cooper's *Gush!* or Martin Amis's *Crude*, many people (especially, but not exclusively, on the left) remain fascinated by one key counterfactual. Without North Sea oil, could the Thatcherite revolution, which so radically altered Britain, have taken place? Harvie notes

---

* The last time I took my children to the seaside, I pulled up 1) the *Shipping Forecast* and 2) the Safer Seas and Rivers Service app, the brainchild of Surfers Against Sewage. Its red and green spots, showing where shit is or is not pumping into our waters, may not yet have the cultural resonance of the *Shipping Forecast*, but we owe its creators a debt almost as large as the one we owe Robert FitzRoy.

wryly: 'In the game of musical chairs, Thatcher had landed on one with a particularly deep velvet cushion.' And it was, speculated Denis Healey, Labour deputy leader in 1980–3, a cushion she sorely needed. 'Without it, she would never have won even her second term; Britain would have been bankrupt by 1983.' Sour grapes? Maybe. His trick at the economic helm did strand Labour on a political desert island – but the numbers certainly bear him out. At its peak, roughly one in every £12 the government took in tax revenues came from the oil industry. (Today, that's down to one in every £100.)

The oil boom also pushed up the value of the pound – a good thing, you might think, after that embarrassing sterling crisis? Unfortunately, the strong pound came at a time when other export industries (e.g. cars, ships, steel, textiles) were already struggling to compete with new players in the Far East, and the exchange rate only made their goods more expensive. One after another, factories closed, destroying hundreds of thousands of jobs. Unemployment doubled. But the magic oil money-tree meant Thatcher could a) pay the welfare bill and b) still cut taxes – or, in the words of the *Telegraph*, 'fund battles against the unions and prop up day-to-day finances'.

But if great tracts of soon-to-be post-industrial Britain were plunged into a deep depression, the oil industry wasn't only a godsend for Margaret Thatcher. At a time when so many other blue-collar jobs were vanishing across Scotland and the north of England, offshore work offered a brave new world of opportunity, even if you'd left school with no qualifications. Yes, it was dangerous, demanding and potentially damaging, but the financial rewards were very appealing.

Al Alvarez, the poet and essayist who has written brilliantly on, among other things, poker, suicide and mountaineering, toured the new oil rigs and wrote up his experiences in *Offshore*. He had a great deal of respect for the 'hard-looking' men, who laboured for the oil industry, which, he said, had given Britain 'something it lost when it gave up its colonies – a frontier'. The trouble, he acknowledged, started when they came back onshore – to the 'beach', to home. Often, like deep-sea divers returning to the surface, they struggled to equalise. 'One of the few releases,' so Alvarez's interlocutors told him, 'from all that tension is a good, old-fashioned, forty-eight hour piss-up. But try explaining that to the missus.'

He visited one rig in the company of Gill, a beautiful woman who worked in PR for Shell. The men weren't used to seeing women offshore. It was, he said, like accompanying Helen around the ramparts of Troy. Not that there was anything to worry about, he says. The men didn't say anything rude or demeaning. Gill, though, clearly didn't feel the same way. She took her lunch tray to the furthest corner of the mess hall and sat with her back to the room. Says Alvarez: 'We ate in silence, and when we finished she walked out of the mess with her eyes down and shoulders hunched defensively.' The men, he said, weren't being lustful – only wistful. He might have felt differently had the men been looking at him. He might have chosen to remember how much the Trojans hated Helen; how much Helen hated herself.

How much has changed in the intervening years is moot. Tabitha Lasley's *Sea State*, published in 2021, was meant to be a piece of reportage on the North Sea oil industry, but it evolved into a much more personal memoir. To her, Aberdeen felt like 'a Gulf state, a desert caliphate': she rarely saw women out alone after dark. In a bar, she bridled at one man's rudeness, only to be told she needed to toughen up: the rules were different offshore, that was how 'lads' talked. Later, watching young men at the airport on crew-change day, she guessed they'd mostly grown up in the northern towns and cities hollowed out by Thatcherite reforms: 'They had a questing look about them; country lads off to seek their fortune, kit bags slung over their shoulders like bindles.'

We ask a lot of those young men. We ask them to work in hard, dangerous, lonely jobs, jobs that alienate them from normal life. We then ask them to come home and pretend that hardness, that danger, that loneliness hasn't touched them. In *Stiffed: The Roots of Modern Male Rage*, a study of the decline in blue-collar work in the US, the feminist author Susan Faludi reminds us that men can feel just as boxed in by society's gendered expectations as women do, but we – wrongly, she says – tell them not to complain. 'The box is there to showcase the man, not to confine him. After all, didn't he build it – and can't he destroy it if he pleases, if he is a *man*.' When women complain about the wife-and-mother box, we call it 'laudable political protest', but when men do the same, we call it 'childish and indecent whining'. Kings, we tell them, shouldn't complain about their castles.

Over the coming decades, we're going to be decommissioning a lot of oil castles in the North Sea, and trade unions want to know what's going to happen to the men (and women; though the percentage working full-time offshore is minuscule) whose jobs are at risk.* The new Labour government, with an eye on its net-zero commitments, has said it won't be issuing any new drilling licences, and without new exploration the existing wells will inevitably dry up.

---

* Tabitha Lasley asked one guy what would become of the rigs when the oil ran out. He laughed, said prisons, maybe.

There is one obvious answer: the new clean green castles of the offshore wind industry. HUMBER has set its sights on becoming Britain's 'green-energy estuary'. Grimsby is already the busiest port for offshore wind servicing in Europe. A giant wind-farm being built on the DOGGER bank could one day power six million homes a year. Aberdeen, too, is poised to pivot from oil to wind, carbon capture and hydrogen. The proof, let's just say, will be in the pudding. For now, let's wish the offshore workers FORTIES, variable 0–3, fair, good, so the helicopters can fly them safely back home to their families. And a hundred years hence, when men and women are tending our North Sea wind farms, we'll hopefully all be singing hallelujahs to West Wind. He'll be keeping our lights on.

SOLO

No man is an island

John Donne, 'Meditation XVII' (1624)

THE *SHIPPING FORECAST* IS A MAD NESOPHILE, naming more areas after islands than anything else. We could say that's just because islands are handy topographical markers and have done with it, but it'd much more fun to say that islands turn everything – spirituality, eccentricity, radicalism, reaction, anarchy, poverty, privilege, *anything* – up to 11. Or, to pinch the excellent words of Judith Schalansky in her intro to *Atlas of Remote Islands*: 'An island offers a stage: everything that happens on it is practically forced to turn into a story, into a chamber piece in the middle of nowhere, into the stuff of literature.'

~~REBEL~~ HORROR ISLAND

A hundred or so years after Julius Caesar didn't conquer us, his great-great-nephew* Claudius found himself, to his own

---

* By adoption: Julius Caesar adopted Octavian, who became the Emperor Augustus, who was Claudius's great-uncle.

and everyone else's surprise, emperor of Rome – an emperor with a serious PR problem. His subjects had him pegged as a feeble, indecisive, hen-pecked cuckold, who preferred reading books to watching gladiators shred each other, which was terrible optics for the job he'd landed. He was, however, by no means stupid. He calculated that succeeding (or sending others to succeed) where Julius Caesar had failed might prove he was a REAL MAN™ after all.

The invasion, says the historian Tacitus, started off well, but the Britons were fighting back from a secret rebel base on the island of Anglesey in the IRISH SEA. The Roman army crossed the Menai Strait, expecting to do battle with other REAL MEN™, only to be transfixed by the barbarous sight of freakish druids, raining down curses on their heads. Worse still, wild, black-robed, unkempt women were running up and down, screaming and brandishing torches, which was very triggering for the sensitive Romans, who'd grown up hearing scary stories about vengeful Furies and blood-mad Maenads, and were absolutely terrified of the chthonic forces of female darkness. General Suetonius Paulinus had to bellow at his legionaries to *man* up. Finally, they mustered the courage to charge.

After the battle, the victorious Romans cut down the island's sacred groves where, according to Tacitus, they found altars festooned with entrails, evidence of druidical atrocities, proof that the rebels were inhuman barbarians who *deserved* to be subjugated. (Not a bit like the Romans, who were, as we know, ever so fastidious when it came to death as public spectacle.) The novel *Imperial Governor*, a stoutly pro-Roman retelling by a British ex-army officer, published in the sixties, really soups it up: 'Over the remains of an enormous fire whose embers still glowed evilly in that dark place hung a wicker cage. Within the scorched framework was a blackened, coagulated mess. An acrid stench thickened the air and closed our throats.'

You might recognise that cage. It debuted in Julius Caesar's war stories, which included a rare contemporary account of the ancient Celtic priesthood. To be fair to him, he did cover their interest in nature, astrology and the transmigration of souls – before getting down to the gory detail his urbane readers really wanted. Druids, he wrote, liked to weave giant figures out of branches, pen their victims inside them, and burn them to a crisp.

Nineteen centuries later, on a different island, the cage reached its apotheosis. In the wake of the sixties youth-quake, the groovier end of our cultural discourse had become less pro-Roman, more pro-druid, keen to back the hairy rebs over the suited-and-booted legions of law and order. Cut to: *The Wicker Man*, a 1973 folk-horror classic, which pits a policeman, very much an avatar of the Man, against the people of Summerisle, an imaginary pagan island in the HEBRIDES. The women are blonde and inviting, rather than ghoulish and bedraggled, and every bit as sinister. But where the General Paulinus succeeded, Sergeant Neil Howie spectacularly fails. Instead of leading the islanders back to the light of civilisation, he winds up being – if you don't already know, I'm not going to spoil it!

Horror can, it seems, bubble up inside any person, any group, any society, any nation, any empire – on any island. When three fine, upstanding British lads, Ralph, Jack and Peterkin, heroes of the high-Victorian boys-own adventure story *The Coral Island*, are squeezed through the looking glass of William Golding's imagination, they become Jack, Ralph and Piggy, the three boys you'll remember in desperate free-fall in *The Lord of the Flies*. Law and order, democracy and fairness, tolerance and decency, descend into fire, fury, blood-lust and slaughter. At the end, Ralph weeps for 'the end of innocence, the darkness of man's heart'. A naval officer, in white drill, with epaulettes and gilt buttons, watches, embarrassed, while Ralph sobs: *he*, of course, would never have stooped so low.

H̶O̶L̶Y̶ EGO ISLAND

The Romans might have cleansed the druids from their island fastness, but a new British spiritual elite – brimful of Christian Kool-Aid – would also decide to seek solitude offshore. One of the oldest, and certainly the most striking, of these religious retreats stands on Skellig Michael, a 200-metre tall, twin-pinnacled rock, seven miles off the coast in SHANNON. Some time between the sixth and eighth centuries, Irish monks landed, built little drystone cells, and settled down to worship their god in peace, a tradition which, despite Viking raids, endured for half a millennium.*

In *Haven*, the Irish writer Emma Donoghue imagines the lives of the first monks to arrive: a single-minded scholar-priest named Artt, and his two increasingly disillusioned companions, young Trian and old Cormac. At first, the three men are excited to be sailing west, away from the sins of the world. After five days of everything the *Shipping Forecast* can throw at them, wind and rain, flat calm and fog, the island appears after Mass on the Sabbath: 'The most gigantic of cathedrals, ready for its priest'. Like Adams on

---

* I was convinced I'd climbed it. I'd even written, 'I went ashore in 2004, a blue summer's day.' But when my mother dug out her diary, there it was: 'Tuesday, 15 June, 2004. Beat towards the Skelligs. Little S. white with gannet shit. Skellig Michael covered w. tourists with boats standing off. Photoed the beehives from below but thought the magic was better preserved by not being ashore.' Funny the tricks memory plays.

a rocky Eden, they marvel at the innocence of the birds – before eating them. *My island*, whispers Artt to himself. *This island's mine.*

As I read, I was wondering who was going to die; somebody always dies at the end of act four. But in this case, it wasn't somebody, but some*thing*. Artt hacks down a rowan tree to make a cross for their chapel. Brother Trian is heart-stopped, devastated. It was the only tree on the island – and not just any tree. The rowan is a potent symbol of nature magic, of ancient spirituality, of a power, call it Celtic, call it druidical, that is antithetical to the Christian god; a god whose Bible Artt has been forcing the illiterate Trian to copy with numb fingers and a hungering belly.

The Scottish poet Kathleen Jamie, in a provocative essay titled 'A Lone Enraptured Male', says those early monks, who sought remote places as part of a spiritual quest, paved the way for how we interact with wild places. 'Literature began with them, and a tradition developed which has persisted ever since and remains largely uninterrogated: the association of literature, remoteness, wildness and spiritually uplifted men.'

The writer Adam Nicolson inherited just such a wild place, the Shiant Islands in HEBRIDES, when he was 21. He has since taken pains to chart his own rejection of monkish solipsism. In his twenties, he writes in *Sea Room*, the Shiants had been 'somewhere to escape from a fretful marriage and from a fretful job in a publishers' office'. Come middle age, he saw solitude as a diminished rather than a heightened state; the islands were not 'Wagnerian stage scenery, lumps of rock in a hostile sea, beside which the solitary hero could exquisitely expire.' In fact, unchecked nesophilia, he thinks, can be a symptom of immaturity, a turning away from the complexities of the real world to a much simpler place, where choices are straightforward and rewards obvious.'

Luke Skywalker, who inherits the fate of the galaxy while still in his teens, would understand. In *The Last Jedi*, old, bearded and monkish, he retreats to Skellig Michael (a.k.a. the planet Ahch-To), home to a mysterious library of sacred books. There, guilt-ridden by his failure to expunge evil from the universe, he is waiting to die. No such luck: young Rey arrives in the *Millennium Falcon* and begs him to leave his sacred isle, to return to the real world and fight. He more or less refuses. She leaves. Nevertheless, shaken by the memories she's stirred up, he turns against the old book-learning. He advances on the library, brandishing a torch: 'I'm going to burn it down.' And when, at the last moment, he hesitates, up steps blue-spirit-Yoda, who incinerates the Jedi texts with a mighty thunderbolt.

'Page-turners,' he says, 'they were not.' Luke, incorporeally at least, finds the courage to leave the island after all.

SHAKESPEARE O.G. ISLAND

The ultimate island-as-stage, where the action of William Shakespeare's *The Tempest* takes place, has no name. It is just – Prospero's. The elderly magician and his daughter Miranda fled there from 'Milan' after his brother usurped his dukedom. Twelve years later, Prospero and his otherworldly sidekick, Ariel, conjure up the eponymous tempest, wrecking a ship carrying the same brother and an assortment of his friends, including a handsome young love interest for Miranda. In one classic production (starring Patrick Stewart of *Star Trek* fame, inked with Inuit tattoos), the action opened with the *Shipping Forecast* crackling storm warnings across the auditorium, the radio ferrying us to this new world.

One of the survivors, a worthy old counsellor called Gonzalo (a nicer version of *Hamlet*'s Polonius), now safe on dry land, falls into a utopian reverie, dreaming of the fresh start an island can offer. *Tabula rasa*! A better life!* 'No use of metal, corn, or wine, or oil; / No occupation; all men idle, all; / And women too, but innocent and pure;

---

* By way of historical context, the Pilgrim Fathers set off for New England within a decade of *The Tempest*'s first performance in 1611.

/ No sovereignty—' But no sooner are we nodding along – tranquillity, innocence, nature, *lovely* – than Gonzalo's mates start to rib him, saying, no kings apart from *you*, right? You'd still be boss, *right?*

Because, of course, before the island was Prospero's, it was home to the indefinably monstrous Caliban, son of Sycorax the witch (who'd have got on with the women of ancient Anglesey like a house on fire). Prospero has enslaved Caliban, but Caliban still insists to anyone who'll listen that the island is *his*: 'As I told thee before, I am subject to a tyrant, a sorcerer, that by his cunning hath cheated me of the island.' And so, with thrust and counter-parry, Shakespeare displays his freakish ability to skewer our fantasies, our hypocrisies. No island is ever truly *ours*.

~~DESERT~~ PIRATE ISLAND

Well-versed though I am in Usborne's *Robinson Crusoe: Young Reading (Series 2)*, I thought I'd better pull up Daniel Defoe's actual text on Gutenberg. In my familiar filleted version, you get to the inciting incident, the shipwreck that lands him on his desert island, on page 2. But it turned out that the uncut version included an awfully loooong build-up. I was about to scroll ahead, when one particular sub-plot caught my eye. Crusoe is at sea, somewhere between the Canary Islands and the coast of Africa, i.e.

just south of TRAFALGAR, when his ship is surprised by a 'Turkish rover' who piled on sail and gave chase. After a brief exchange of cannon fire, Crusoe's ship is boarded, overpowered, and he is taken to Sallee, where he spends two years as a 'miserable slave'.

For Salle, I discovered, read Salé, which lies north of Rabat on the Atlantic coast of Morocco. Today it's a commuter town; in Crusoe's time (the 1650s) it was a city-state, a corsair republic, the westernmost output of Barbary piratedom, which is itself a catch-all term for men who, with state approval, put out from the North African littoral to attack European shipping. In other words, from the POV of the Ottoman-backed rulers of Algiers, Tunis, and Tripoli, the Barbary pirates weren't pirates – they were privateers.

But of course, from the POV of the men, women and children living and working in the south and west of Britain and Ireland, the Barbary pirates *were* pirates, and totally and utterly terrifying. With raids happening almost daily, coastal traders and fishermen didn't want to put to sea, for fear of leaving their families at the mercy of hit-and-run slavers. As Sir John Eliot, the Vice-Admiral of Devon, admitted: 'The seas around England seem'd theirs.' In the 1620s and 1630s, some corsairs were even bold enough to use LUNDY, now a mild-mannered island in the Bristol

Channel, as a convenient hideout, right under the nose of the British authorities.

Throughout the seventeenth century and well into the eighteenth, thousands of people were plucked from boats or villages, belying – or rather illuminating – James Thomson's 1740 lyrics to 'Rule Britannia'. Britons, in large numbers, very much *were* slaves. Their lives, however, remain largely undocumented, their fates largely unknown. Many died – of disease, of punishment, of over-work. A *tiny* minority foreswore Christianity and found ways to prosper. Some were ransomed. Others, like Robinson Crusoe, escaped.

Crusoe, though, experienced zero cognitive dissonance when, a free man once more, he set himself up in business in Brazil and ventured back to the west coast of Africa to *buy enslaved people* – the journey on which he (karmically?) was eventually shipwrecked. Linda Colley, whose book *Captives* is a sensitive and sophisticated study of how Britons in the age of empire didn't always have the upper hand *vis-à-vis* non-Europeans, reminds us that our society as a whole had a similar blind spot. Reflecting on the Barbary threat, she writes: 'only a minority of Britons seem to have acknowledged any parallel between their own risk of being captured at sea by North African corsairs, and the much greater threat that British slaving ventures increasingly posed to men and women in West Africa.'

Ironically, once the navy got its act together, and the likelihood of being captured by pirates diminished, so the appetite for stories *about* pirates grew exponentially. In 1724, Captain Charles Johnson (possibly a pseudonym for Defoe, who frankly makes Miss Rabbit look lazy) published *A General History of the Robberies and Murders of the Most Notorious Pyrates*, which sketched out the parameters for the now classic cosmos of skulls, crossbones and elaborate beards. Crucially, the stars of this show were a) largely from Britain or Ireland and b) largely operating in the Caribbean and Indian Ocean, i.e. far away from home.

The American anthropologist and anarchist activist David Graeber, in his book *Pirate Enlightenment*, goes so far as to say such accounts of exotic, remote pirate islands may have constituted a form of 'poetic expression' for the emerging North Atlantic proletariat, who lapped up this glamorous, gritty otherworld where crime paid. Pirate crews, he said, were diverse *avant la lettre*, which made them naturally committed to 'a certain rough-and-ready egalitarianism'. You could even, he writes, consider pirate islands as 'perfect laboratories of democratic experiment'.

Today, the Bristol Channel is a quiet sort of place, and nobody braving the lumpy crossing to LUNDY expects to find a den of iniquity or the beating heart of any kind of revolution. Even a travel guide published more than a century ago remarked: 'Life on Lundy is said to be very dull now; but this is the fault of our over-sensitive modern morality.' I'd like to pretend a pirate's life is the life for me, but I'm quite happy to sign up for nothing riskier than a weekend in the lighthouse cottage, with a bottle of rum and a stack of good books.

~~VILLAIN~~ LITERARY ISLAND

Bond villains eat islands for breakfast. Dr No and his metal hands, Scaramanga and his golden gun, Largo and his eye patch, Stromberg and his mate Jaws, Lyutsifer Safin and his nano-bots; island-mad, the lot of them. They *are* piratical, often anarchic, but I don't *think* anyone is going to hold them up as model revolutionaries. Traditionally, the Bond villain has eschewed *Shipping Forecast* waters, preferring tropical weather. One story, though, does place a baddie bent on world domination on one of our home islands: T. H. White's *The Master*, a children's book set on ROCKALL.*

It was published in 1957, when Ian Fleming would have been writing *Dr No*, and two years after Britain staked its claim (brass plaque plus Union Jack) to this

---

* A small gift for those of ~~you~~ us who have yet to accept that Middle Earth isn't a real place: the underwater topographical features around ROCKALL include Lorien Knoll and Isengard Ridge, the Fangorn and Edoras Banks, and the Rohan and Gondor Seamounts. You are, as they say, welcome.

most small and unprepossessing of territories. You might imagine that a 20-metre-high rock, more or less in the middle of nowhere, was neither here nor there. But back then, we were worried that the Soviets might perch on ROCKALL and spy on us when we practising with our new nuclear weapons.

In the novel, a twin brother and sister become trapped inside the Master's island lair, which T. H. White (better known for *The Sword in the Stone*; one biographer calls the Master 'a bleak replacement of Merlyn') populates with a cast of queasy stereotypes. He does, however, cunningly deploy the *Shipping Forecast* to show us how very, *very* far the children are from home. 'That evening, an educated voice* from the warm rooms of a radio station would be using the familiar phases about ROCKALL MALIN HEBRIDES'.

We don't need to worry about the plot (mind control, vibrator-rays), especially as it hinges on a) the goodies trying to rescue their dog to get the plot going and b) the baddie tripping over the same dog to tie things up. In fact, White doesn't seem bothered about the plot either, being more interested in cramming in as many references to *The Tempest* as possible. As children said in the 1950s: *whizzo*.

---

* See POETRY for what the avowedly working-class MP John Prescott has to say about that educated voice.

~~PATRIOT~~ POISON ISLAND

Cooking up mass-murder on remote islands doesn't just belong to stories. When my brother and I were no older than the children in *The Master*, our parents took us sailing in HEBRIDES. On our way to Ullapool, we passed a small, green, low-lying island which, to our jaded eyes, didn't have much to distinguish it from all the other small, green, low-lying islands we'd sampled that holiday. Until, that is, our mother told us that if we so much as set foot on its shores *we ... would ... die*. Why why why? we clamoured. Because it was covered in deadly bacteria that would kill us soon as look at us, *that's why*. For a child brought up in the twilight of the Cold War, fed on a strict diet of apocalyptic fiction, this was bedtime reading crash-landing in reality.

Later, I'd always assumed she was exaggerating – like, there'd been a *tiny* lab there, or something. But no, not a bit of it. Thanks to the power of YouTube, I found a real-life folk-horror film that tells the whole story in excruciate detail. Part of the Imperial War Museum's archive, it's in colour, shaky, silent, with a pukka voiceover. Now declassified, it was originally put together at Porton Down, the top-secret research lab, from footage shot by a US observer (who must have thought we were off our rockers).

In the dark days between Dunkirk and D-Day, we were casting around desperately for ways to beat Hitler. Over in

Los Alamos, Oppenheimer and co. were working on their destroyer-of-worlds A-bomb. In HEBRIDES, by contrast, we were hatching a cunning plan to ... poison all the German cows.* And since practice makes perfect, scientists chose lucky Gruinard as the base for their biological warfare field-trials. Part of me still can't believe I've not been duped by some elaborate hoax, but here goes.

You watch soldiers bundling sheep onto boats. You watch them unloading sheep and bundling them into 'exposure' crates (yes, *exactly* like sacrificial druid cages). You watch them waiting for an offshore i.e. easterly wind, so it's safe to carry out the trials. They blast a cloud of anthrax at the sheep. They unbox the sheep and tether them in long lines. Some sheep get away. 'Anyone who believes sheep are docile and slow-moving should try catching† them, particularly if he's wearing full protective clothing,' chuckles the voiceover, genially. We watch, we wait. On the third day, the sheep start to die. Dead sheep are eviscerated and inspected. The trials are pronounced a huge success.

A vote of thanks, I say, to the D-Day weather forecasters.

---

* Serendipitous footnote: Sir Oliver Graham Sutton, the man in charge of so-called Operation Vegetarian (no comment), went on to head up the Met Office.
† Pronounced 'ketching'.

GRUINARD ISLAND
THIS ISLAND IS
GOVERNMENT PROPERTY
UNDER EXPERIMENT.
THE GROUND IS CONTAMINATED
WITH ANTHRAX AND DANGEROUS.
LANDING IS PROHIBITED.
BY ORDER 1986

~~PIRATE~~ POSTMODERN ISLAND

The generation which came of age after the Second World War thought the music BBC radio played was square; a real drag. Where could they hear the new 'rock 'n' roll', the new 'pop'? The BBC was a monopoly broadcaster: there were no commercial radio stations. Come the sixties, a few enterprising individuals (including Screaming Lord Sutch, the founder of the Official Monster Raving Loony Party) had a very bright idea. Why not set up their own radio stations? They couldn't do this on dry land, but what about on boats anchored offshore – or, even better, on one of the deserted forts which peppered the Thames Estuary?

In 1965 'Paddy' Roy Bates, who'd already had his fair share of war-time adventures, took his 12-year-old boy Michael on an unusual father–son outing. They motored out to a fort called Knock John and, with the tide sucking and surging round its base, clambered up a dodgy old ladder onto the platform. They scoped out the joint, watched over by cormorants, and Bates decided it'd be the perfect spot. Radio Essex began broadcasting in 1965. Unfortunately, the rozzers did not dig their far-out music, and because Knock John was technically inside UK territorial waters, a year later Bates found himself up before the beak, fined and gagged – but he didn't give up. He scouted another fort, Roughs Tower, which, at some

7.5 nautical miles off Harwich, was (as the law then stood) in international waters. Bates boarded the fort, kicked off a band of other wannabe radio-pirates (right in the middle of their Christmas dinner) and got down to business.

Determined to stick it to the Man, Bates announced the foundation of the Principality of Sealand, an independent state with him as its king. That wound the Man up no end. The British government, according to the micro-nation's official history, was so paranoid about having some sort of 'Cuba off the east coast of England' that it sent in the military to blow up all the other forts. A navy ship buzzed Sealand, shouting, 'You're next!' Prince Michael fired a pistol shot across the bow, but when the Man tried to take him and his dad to court on firearms charges, the ruling came down in their favour. The English court had no jurisdiction. Sealand was *terra nullius*. No man's land. *Their* land.

And they were prepared to fight for it. Ten years later, Prince Michael was alone on Sealand while his parents were in Austria on state business – which turned out to be a ruse designed to lure them away from the fort. A helicopter dropped some of Prince Roy's erstwhile German business partners on the tower. They locked Michael up, threatened to throw him overboard, and finally shipped him to Holland. Somehow, he snuck back into the UK without a passport and joined the epic fight-back. The Sealand royal family procured a helicopter. They levered off its doors, rounded up rope, guns and ammo, and went in at dawn. The raid was a complete success – as witnessed by the *Sun*, which had hired a boat to report on the original coup, only to arrive and discover the Bates family were ascendant once more. The newspaper ran its scoop, complete with a photo of the (amusingly, if you were a *Sun* sub) German prisoners.

Sealand – motto: *E Mare Libertas* – is still flying the flag for island freedom today. You don't just sign up to their newsletter. You JOIN THE REVOLUTION! And yet it has borrowed one antediluvian tradition from the UK: with the right amount of cash, you can buy yourself a peerage. The price list, unlike ours, is transparent and affordable. My finger is hovering over *lady* for a very reasonable £19.99. I might wait. If enough of you buy this book, I could ape Prospero and treat myself to a dukedom.

STORY

'I think we shall go on always, like the Flying Dutchman,' said Gwendolen wildly.

George Eliot, *Daniel Deronda* (1876)

THE MOST DISCUSSED BULLETIN in the *Shipping Forecast*'s history was read out at 0015 on Tuesday 14 August, 1979.

I was one and a half, sound asleep in my cot in a village in Somerset, so I can't claim to have heard it. My parents, too, were tucked up in bed. But Aunt Margaret, my namesake, a night owl, was visiting. My mother thinks she was up sewing. She definitely had the radio on. This is what she heard: LUNDY, FASTNET, IRISH SEA, south to southwest veering westerly 7 to severe gale 9, locally storm 10 in FASTNET. She didn't, I'm sure, wait to hear, rain then showers, moderate or good. Instead she ran to my parents' room and shook them awake. My father threw on his clothes, leapt in the car and drove, I hope cautiously, to PLYMOUTH. 'I knew there was going to be trouble,' he told me, 'but I had no the idea of the scale.' My mother, nine months pregnant, stayed behind. It was, you see, thanks to my embryonic brother that they were safely at home, not out there in the dark, battling the sudden storm that ravaged the 1979 Fastnet Race.

Two and a half days earlier, 303 boats had started the race, which runs from WIGHT, round the FASTNET rock off the south coast of Ireland and back to PLYMOUTH, a journey of more than 600 nautical miles. Of those boats, only 86 finished the race. Twenty-four were abandoned, of which five sank. Fifteen people died. It was a disaster that shook the racing community and shocked the nation.

My parents met ocean-racing. My mother's parents used to sail, and she loved it, but they sold up in the early seventies. Then, at a party, she met a man who said he'd go one better: he'd take her *racing*. I believe he tested her arm muscles. This man is *not* my father, though he was my godfather. There weren't, as you can guess, a lot of other women on the scene; I rather suspect my mother did what we'd now call *more than her fair share of cooking*. Still, after one race, their crew was invited for a drink on the boat of some competitors. And there, sitting at the far end of the saloon, right where the mast comes down, scarcely visible through a fog of cigarette smoke, was my father. It was, she said, love at first sight. * They married in 1974, the year

---

* She has since corrected me. It was *fancy* at first sight.

the *Shipping Forecast* turned 50, honeymooning in Scotland on the boat they'd bought. In the 1975 FASTNET race, they came second (adjusted for handicap: *Polar Bear* was only 34 feet long), which for amateur sailors was frankly about as good as it gets.

Offshore racing was a different beast back then. Primarily, there were fewer professional sailors and fewer sponsored boats. The tech was also totally different: no GPS, for starters. Once you lost sight of land, you had to figure out where you were by dead reckoning, which is educated guesswork; or by getting a bearing off radio beacons, which is nauseatingly fiddly; or by getting a bearing off the sun or stars, which is a high-stakes maths test. As for weather information, most people relied entirely on the *Shipping Forecast*. Thanks to the BBC's long-wave signal, this extended far out to sea, and it'd also be relayed by the coastguard on VHF radio (although back then only two-thirds of the fleet carried one). But, as we saw with the Great Storm of 1987, forecasting was nothing like as fine-grained as it is now: depressions could arrive suddenly and deepen rapidly.

When the fleet sailed out of Cowes on Saturday 11 August, the forecast was benign. Two days later, there was still nothing alarming: southwesterly 4 or 6, increasing 6 or 7 for a time, what you'd call a good racing breeze.

But at tea-time the same day, Radio 4 interrupted its programming to broadcast a force 8 gale warning, which was repeated in the scheduled forecast at 1750. For racing sailors, force 8 wasn't a dealbreaker. I asked my dad (who, remember, preaches the gospel of the prudent mariner) what he'd have done if he'd heard it. 'I'd have made sure everything was secure. I'd have rehearsed how to get the storm jib on. I'd have looked at how the wind was going shift to make sure we were on the best tack.' Would he have run for land? 'For a force 8? No.'

An hour later, Radio 4 broke off again, upping the gale warning to force 9, which might – *might* – have made some of the smaller boats think twice about carrying on. The trouble was, they didn't hear it. Nobody kept Radio 4 on non-stop at sea. Another unscheduled gale warning followed at 2300: southwesterly severe gale force 9, increasing storm force 10, imminent. Again, most of the boats didn't hear it. And when, finally, the fleet tuned in for the scheduled broadcast after midnight, the warning which had so alarmed my Aunt Margaret was no longer a surprise: the storm had already hit.

When, later that night, my dad arrived at the Royal Ocean Racing Club base at the finish line, he realised he was the one of the most senior members ashore. A man from the local yacht club came up to him and said: 'People are dying out there. What are you going to do about it?' In the aftermath, again and again, the press asked the same question: why didn't the race organisers call off the race? Two problems. One: there was no way to tell the sailors the race was off; the communication technology didn't exist. Two: even if they'd been able to, it wouldn't have made any difference. The fleet was far out at sea. Nobody was going to run for land in a storm. In bad weather you *stay out*. However bad a storm is at sea, a storm close to land, in shallower water, in bad visibility, without GPS or radar, is much, *much* worse. 'Chatter like this,' writes John Rousmaniere, journalist and author of the compelling account *Fastnet, Force 10*, who took part in the race, 'boils up from easy chairs whenever bad weather hits. Some people are always under the impression that blowing a whistle will magically transport the vessels and their crews out of the tempest to a safe haven'.

Barry O'Donnell, an Irish paediatric surgeon, who also served as chair of the *British Medical Journal*, wrote a deadpan account – almost an anti-story – of his own experience of the race, skippering a young crew, which included his two teenage sons. The barometer, he said, started to fall as his boat passed Land's End on the Monday morning, dropping an 'unbelievable' 40mb in 24 hours. By 11pm they were down to bare poles, i.e. the wind was too strong for them to carry any sail at all – and that was before they'd heard any serious gale warning at all. He got his crew together down below and told them they weren't going to abandon ship. 'I had no mutiny because I was so much older than them all and we had no problems, no hysteria – there were at least two boats in which crew members had to be struck, but mine wasn't one of them.' He told his boys the boat wouldn't sink. To which his 15-year-old replied: 'He sounds like the skipper of the Titanic.'*

It *was* frightening, O'Donnell wrote. The force-12 gusts *were* terrifying. Each oncoming wave *was* so vast it blacked out everything else. Two of the crew *were* swept overboard, only to be saved by their belt-and-braces harness and safety line. But at the same time he hoped his son wouldn't be propping up a yacht club bar in 50 years' time (i.e. right about now), foot on rail, G&T in hand, telling anyone who'd listen, 'You don't know what it was like – it was hell out there.' Why not? Because, he says: 'The Fastnet race in 1979 showed that sailing is not an *absolutely* safe sport.' In fact, the chance

---

* Staying on board was the right call, though. Four people died when their life-rafts capsized or broke up. That was the most important lesson to draw from the RORC's report (written by my mother's mother): so long as a boat is afloat, don't leave it. The vast majority of abandoned boats were later found drifting safely.

to pit themselves against bad weather – just not *that* bad – was why some people went to sea in the first place. 'The challenge of sailing through rough weather,' confirms Rousmaniere, 'is indisputably one of the attractions of ocean racing.'

Many yachts, when they don't need to strip out every ounce of weight for racing, have a little library of classic sailing stories on board, tucked on a shelf in the saloon, with a bungee-cord or wooden baton stopping them falling out when the boat heels. You meet the same volumes over and over again. Joshua Slocum's account of becoming the first person to sail (slowly and carefully) around the world alone – although he does occasionally keep company with a friendly ghost. Captain Cook's pioneering voyages. Earnest Shackleton's Antarctic epic. Books called scary things like *Survive the Savage Sea* or *Adrift*. A volume or two of Mike Peyton cartoons. They're like disparate parts of one amorphous sailing bible. They teach; they warn. But they also beckon. They are, in their own funny, old-fashioned, gruff way, like so many sirens on so many rocks. The sweetest songs, I've found, are about the men who first sailed (or tried to sail) around the world alone, non-stop, running before the winds and waves of the Southern Ocean, where storm 10 is nothing to write home about. Everyone on that tragic FASTNET race, I can almost guarantee, would have known their names, read their stories – maybe even dreamed of emulating them.

In fact, when I (briefly) found myself underwater on a yacht in the Pacific, a hundred miles from land, in a force 10 storm, I'd say those books were part of the reason I was there. When the breaking cross-sea reared up to port, 20, 30, 40, god only knows how many feet high, in that frozen moment of time before we were knocked flat, a part of me recognised it, a part of me thought, aaaaah, there you are, I've been waiting for you.

Let's go back the 1960s. The heroic feats of the Second World War were gone, but not forgotten. Everest had been climbed. The Americans were off to the moon. And in 1966 a 64-year-old British yachtsman called Francis Chichester set out from England in an ordinary-looking boat called *Gipsy Moth IV* to sail around the world. He was planning to leave the Cape of Good Hope to port, stop once in Australia, before continuing across the Southern Ocean, where the West Wind rules even more monomaniacally than he does in the north. In those latitudes, there's no land to moderate his power: that's why we call them the Roaring Forties, the Furious Fifties, the Screaming Sixties. If Chichester made it all the way to

Cape Horn, he'd turn left, and sail up the Atlantic – and home. When he returned to PLYMOUTH in 1967, nine months and a day after setting off, his achievement blew the nation's mind.

There's an iconic set of photos, snapped from the decks of HMS *Protector* as Chichester rounded Cape Horn. *Gypsy Moth IV* is heavily reefed, the mizzenmast bare, only scraps of jib on the forestay. 'Just then,' wrote Chichester afterwards, 'I'm damned if an aircraft didn't buzz into sight. I cursed it. If there was one place in the world where I expected to be alone it was off Cape Horn'.*

A cheering crowd, thousands strong, greeted him in London, perhaps surprised by the slight figure he cut, by his thick glasses, by his modest schoolmasterly air. But looks can be deceiving. Before the war, he'd been a pioneering solo aviator, and had been devastated when his poor eyesight ruled him out of a combat role. And now, in peacetime, he reminded everyone of Britain's glory days. 'He was,' wrote the journalist J. R. L. Anderson in an epilogue to Chichester's own account, 'the nation's hero, but to me he seemed to epitomise not scarlet and lace, but that incredible endurance

---

* According to a journalist on board that aircraft, the Chilean pilot, who I like to imagine was hard to impress, muttered, '*Muy hombre.*'

that the people of England have shown when it was needed of them'.* In a blaze of mutually beneficial PR, Elizabeth II knighted him with the same sword which Elizabeth I had used to knight Sir Francis Drake after he captained the first English ship to circumnavigate the globe (slowly, with a large crew and breaks for plundering).

To those crowds, it was a brilliant feat, an uplifting story. To other serious sailors, it meant something rather different. Now, there was only one thing left to do. Sail around the world. Single-handed. *Non-stop.*

The *Sunday Times* could smell a story, and it swiftly laid down the Golden Globe challenge, which was part-race, part-stunt. Basically, any boat that set off between 1 June and 31 October 1968, and made it round the world and back, would be in the running for two cash prizes, one for first, one for fastest. It wasn't really a race because, frankly, nobody knew whether one man and one boat could withstand the mental and physical battering of all those months at sea. As Robin Knox-Johnston, who provided the world with the definitive answer, wrote much later: 'These days, when people are thundering round the world in purpose-built greyhounds in less than 100 days, it is hard to fully

---

* I'm reading from my parents' musty 1967 edition, published in November, already reprinted in December, a small clue as to quite what an impact he made.

appreciate that [...] we were not even sure a non-stop circumnavigation was possible.'*

For Knox-Johnston, getting there first was a point of national as well as merely personal pride. A Frenchman, you see, called Eric Tabarly had recently won a major single-handed transatlantic race. *Paris Jour* had crowed: 'Thanks to him it is the French flag that triumphs in the longest and most spectacular race on that ocean which the Anglo-Saxons consider as their special domain.' Knox-Johnston felt this very keenly: 'By rights a Briton should do it first, and in the circumstances he had better get moving.' That *by rights* speaks volumes, doesn't it? Peter Nichols, in his buy-it-now account of the race, *A Voyage for Madmen*, describes Knox-Johnston as an 'unfashionable, almost eccentrically square young man from another era', although perhaps not everyone swung as much in the sixties as we like to think they did. *Get moving*, though, he certainly did. In June 1968, he put to sea in the diminutive *Suhaili*, and 312 days later he showed the world that sailing was coming home.

But there was another competitor who very much did embody the Age of Aquarius. Bernard Moitessier was

---

* For context, so we don't get blasé, maybe 200 people have matched his achievement. That's fewer than the 280-odd who've been to the International Space Station, and the 800-odd who've summited K2.

French, but he didn't sail for the glory of France; he saved
his love for Vietnam, the old French colony of Indochina,
where he'd spent a barefoot childhood learning to sail
with fishermen in the Gulf of Siam. In his boat, *Joshua*,
named in honour of the single-handed pioneer Joshua
Slocum, he'd already sailed happily around Cape Horn,
having decided it was the 'logical route' from Polynesia
to Paris. (He and his wife were hurrying to collect their
children from school.) No, Moitessier entered the race not
for national glory, but as part of a more personal quest,
and his mesmeric vivid-present account, published as *La
Longue Route* or *The Long Way*, is very much acid on the
beach, not G&Ts at the bar.

His arrival at Cape Horn reads like a reverie. *Joshua*'s
going fast. Moitessier is standing on the deck, a man-boat
chimera, transcendent, blissed out. 'One surfing run
taken the wrong way in the clear night ... and my beautiful bird of the capes would go on her way with the
ghosts in the foam, guided by a seagull or a porpoise.' He
drops the main, reduces sail, slows down, telling himself
to hold tight to his boat and his sanity. The next night,
he slips round the Horn, which was 'pale and tender' in
the moonlight. 'A great cape,' he assures us, 'has a soul,
with very soft, very violent shadows and colours. A soul as
smooth as a child's, as hard as a criminal's. And that is

why we go.' And it was then, with the hardest part of the race safely in his wake, that he made the decision for which he is justly famous.

He didn't turn north. He didn't go left, up the Atlantic and across the finishing line where, almost certainly, he'd have been fastest, and maybe even first. Instead, he thought about what claiming such a prize would mean. It would mean kowtowing to false gods, to the Monster, to Mammon, to the sorts of people who would, in his words, put out the stars to make their billboards shine more brightly at night. He made his call. Using a slingshot (he carried no radio transmitter on principle), he catapulted a message onto the deck of a tanker off the Cape of Good Hope, telling the world, sorry, I'm not your story anymore. He was, he said, going to stay at sea, because he was happy – and also, perhaps, to save his soul. He sailed on, non-stop, to Tahiti, spending 37,455 nautical miles and ten months at sea. In other words, he didn't just sail around the world, alone, non-stop. He sailed around the world, alone, non-stop, *one and a half times*.

Moitessier escaped the Monster. Another competitor wasn't so fortunate. His name was Donald Crowhurst, and he was something of a curio, until two films about his life, *Crowhurst* and *The Mercy*, came out back to back in 2017–18. 'Dreams are the seeds of action. We'd all do well to remember that,' Colin Firth–Donald Crowhurst tells his children during a family outing on a sweet Swallows-and-Amazons dinghy. 'If I can do it, then so can the bloke who stares at the horizon in wonder.' His story is a chilling cautionary tale about how sometimes we don't achieve our dreams, about how sometimes the underdog doesn't triumph.

His wife (in *The Mercy*, although also, we can assume, in real life) tells him his story is already good enough for her. You've built a company. You've got *us*, your family. But that story wasn't big enough for him. He wanted more. And so, despite having only a rudimentary knowledge of shipbuilding and sailing, he got himself up to the eyeballs in debt to join the race, setting sail from Teignmouth on 31 October 1968, the last possible day. To make his money back, he knew he had to sell his story. He knew he had to feed the Monster.

While he was still in the Atlantic, Crowhurst accepted he was never, ever going to make it round alive; he and his gimcrack trimaran, *Teignmouth Electron*, a bodged job, simply weren't up to it. But he couldn't – wouldn't – daren't – turn back. He started to fake his story, radioing in false updates (you couldn't get away with that nowadays), while meandering off the coast of South America. His vain hope was that maybe, just maybe, he could wait until a couple of the others finished, and then he'd slink quietly north, at the back of the pack, an also-ran, and nobody need be any the wiser. But, to his horror, one by one the other competitors dropped out. Knox-Johnston was first, but Crowhurst now ran the risk of being fastest. He'd be found out. Humiliated. Shunned. Ruined. The Monster wouldn't hang out the bunting. It would eat him alive.

His boat was found adrift in July 1969. He was not on board, but his logbooks and charts were there for all to see. Together, they chart his horrible slide from rational fear into a mind-maze of delusion, in which he claimed to understand everything in the world from Julius Caesar to Chairman Mao. One of the last entries reads: 'I am what I am and I see the nature of my offence … It is finished – It is finished – IT IS THE MERCY.' Most people assume he took his own life.

If his story was a cautionary tale then, how much more is it now? Even if the Monster isn't all that interested in you or me, we're constantly being encouraged to appease his minions, the mini-monsters of social media, with titbits of liver and marrow. Under the Monster's scathing eye, we try to hold two stories in our heads at once, a true one for us, an imaginary one for the rest of the world, never mind that the strain risks sending us, like Crowhurst, a little bit mad.

That all happened long before I was born. My turn to watch a sailor navigate the unholy trinity of wind, waves and Monster came in January 2001 when Ellen MacArthur, aged 24, barely a year older than I was, found herself in the lead in Vendée Globe round-the-world race.

The Vendée follows the same route as the original Golden Globe, with a start line in BISCAY, but it takes place on identical boats called Open 60s, which possess a level of technology which would have looked like pure wizardry to earlier generations. Part of that wizardry, for those of us stuck in office jobs (my days were then spent making cups of tea for the nation's most bankable comedy talent), was that we could wait till our bosses were elsewhere, jump online (no internet at home) and scroll frantically for updates. I was obsessed; MacArthur's is a very powerful story.

She was born in Derbyshire, *Shipping Forecast* area NONE. She saved her lunch money to buy her first little keelboat. Glandular fever poleaxed her in her teens. Stuck in bed, watching the Whitbread round-the-world race, she found it difficult to identify with more 'macho' sailors who she felt 'rarely seemed to show any form of sensitivity towards the sea'. She sailed round Britain by herself when she was only 18. She navigated the rocks and shoals of corporate sponsorship and built the sort of team without which twenty-first-century dreams don't come true. She made it to the start aboard *Kingfisher;* she made it round the world; she nearly, *nearly* won.

She rounded Cape Horn in second place, but was soon closing on her rival, Michel Desjoyeaux, sacrificing her second-to-last pack of Ginger Nuts to Neptune when she recrossed the equator, because – praise be! – he was stuck in a windless hole. But then, just as they were neck and neck, she was hit by two fateful mishaps: a submerged container damaged one of her daggerboards and she lost time making repairs, only for a forestay to break, which stopped her carrying maximum sail. 'Mich' outpaced her and won. She came a valiant second – but he remained her friend, even though he's *French*; see what a long way we've come!

That, then, was her story, and although she lost the wind-and-waves battle, she won the Monster war. We admired her openness, her honesty, her disarming normality. We admired how she combined an adamantine grit with human fragility. We could actually relate to her. *Relate*, etymologically speaking, means to *bring back*, and that's what she did. She went down there, down into the Southern Ocean, returned with the hero's elixir, and gave us all a sip. Or that's how it felt to me, minimising my browser when the bosses came back from lunch.

But what's surprising/depressing/not-actually-surprising is that when, a few years later, MacArthur only went and beat the solo round-the-world speed record on board a whopping trimaran, the Monster's reaction was a bit ... snippy? Wrote the *Telegraph*: 'What is a girl who loves the sea, understands the poetry of boats, can weep at the sight of a sunset in the Southern Ocean, doing in such a contraption?' Wasn't it better in the good old days? Knox-Johnston didn't weep into deck-cams. He memorised *poetry*.

People are still racing around the world. Non-stop or in stages. Solo or with a crew. Upwind or downwind. On monohulls or multihulls. As beginners or as pros. You can even do it retro, back-to-basics, cottage-core, with no tech allowed that wasn't around when Chichester and Knox-Johnston wowed the world: no GPS, no autopilot, no water-maker, no Kevlar, no mobile phone, no Kindle, no electronic watch – no nothing. (*The Shipping Forecast*, though? *De riguere!*)

People do still race – but MacArthur doesn't. She's quit professional sailing, and now devotes herself to environmental research and campaigning. She leverages her original story to tell a very different one, one about how we need to stop gobbling up the world's resources as if they were as unending as the Southern Ocean's storms. 'No experience in my life,' she said in a TED Talk about her solo racing days, 'could have given me a better understanding of the definition of the word finite. What we have out there is all we have. There is no more.'

OTHERWORLD

for here, millions of mixed shades and shadows, drowned dreams, somnambulisms, reveries; all that we call lives and souls, lie dreaming, dreaming

Herman Melville, *Moby-Dick; or, The Whale* (1851)

I HAVE A PHOTOGRAPH, taken on Brighton Beach, in late 2001, or maybe early 2002, when the chance reflection of a cloud looks like the whole of Britain is mirrored in the sea. That's our destination now. Not the real world of ports and politics and prizes, but the otherworld rippling in the water.

As sleep in our antsy blue-lit this-world has become more and more fetishised, so the *Shipping Forecast* can be found moonlighting on BBC Sounds in *The Sleeping Forecast*, a swash of soothing music mixed with snatches of FISHER ... fog ... fair.* It is soporific, sedative, both passport and portal to the otherworld of sleep. But to focus on the brass tacks (hot bath, cold room) of sleep hygiene is to forget that the *Shipping Forecast* is also *dreamy*. It's part of the hypnagogia, that strange

---

* Even the greats need a portfolio career these days.

interregnum when we're not quite awake, not quite asleep, when our conscious minds no longer have a firm hand on the tiller of reality, but have yet to quit the deck to take a watch below, when, Iggle-Piggles in our little boats, we cast off from the shores of reality to pitch and yaw on other, darker waters. This neverland is a precious place, and the *Shipping Forecast* is our pilot, our psychopomp, our Charon.

The day-time forecasts belong to the pedestrian world of work and duty and care. The ones we most cleave to come at the liminal hours, at 0048, when true night begins, and at 0520, when night's shadows flee. At sea, on watch on a small boat, you listen to the 0048 forecast lit by the red glow of the light above the chart table, a light soft enough to protect your night vision, before climbing back on deck to sail in darkness beneath the ghost-flap of the ghost-sail. Come 0520, the slow creep of dawn will be underway, and some little grey light will have trickled down below. The crew, humped in their sleeping bags, might stir, might huff and roll, when you flick the radio switch. They're still dreaming – what of? – while you listen to reality's return. You put the kettle on the gimballed stove (as quietly as you can) and think about breakfast, boat chores, the day ahead, light, life, and wait for them to breach.

When we look out to sea, we leave the shallows of our minds behind and start to sift deeper waters, hunting the silver flicker of thoughts and feelings we cannot always catch in our shore-bound lives. When W. G. Sebald, an expert trawler of this otherworld, came across men fishing on the shores of East Anglia, he knew their tents, their gear, tokened something more than hobby, than sport, than leisure: 'It is as if the last stragglers of some nomadic people had settled there, at the outermost limit of the earth, in expectation of the miracle longed for since time immemorial, the miracle which would justify all their erstwhile privations and wanderings.'

The day I took that photograph, my two friends and I had gone to the shore because London had sucked the life out of us. We were scoured, desiccated, hollow. We wanted to look at a horizon, to hear wave-songs, to dream again. Of course, that's not how we put it. *A day out!* we said. *Chips!* we said. But that's what we meant. And when we stood there, on the brink, we stood in the footprints of the Greeks, the Romans, the Vikings, the Celts, of all the many, many people who have, for centuries, felt sure the Atlantic seaboard was a gateway to *something*. They felt that out there, past SOLE, past the western rim of the *Shipping Forecast*, past the monsters, somewhere out there, there might even be paradise.

The Roman poet Horace, a gentle soul compared with many of his contemporaries, wrote at a time of civil war, of political upheaval. The Ocean, so he says in one of his *Epodes*, is waiting for him, and beyond the Ocean lies something worth dreaming of, those rich and fertile lands, the Isles of the Blessed. Once there, he won't need to plough his fields or prune his vines; his olive trees will never fail; there'll be figs, there'll be honey. But there's a catch: his word for *is waiting* sounds very similar to the Latin word for *ghosts*, for *shades*, for *the dead*. Beyond the Ocean, there's a beautiful land, a land of promise, a land with many names –

the Isles of the Blessed   Vinland

  the New World   the Elysian Fields

     Saint Brendan's Isle

   Tír na nÓg   Valinor

      Avalon

       Hy-Brasil

– but sometimes you can only reach it when you're gone.*

---

* The very real westward journeys of men and women, driven from Ireland by famine and from Scotland by the Clearances, took place on what became known, because of grim levels of on-board mortality, as *coffin ships*. Some were vessels which had been repurposed after the abolition of the trade in enslaved people.

In stories, babies are sometimes found drifting in boats (the prophet Moses, the parricide Mordred), and are plucked from death and given life. So too, we have taken the metaphor of a last voyage and turned it into something real. In the curtain-raiser to *Beowulf*, the first 'English' epic, we say farewell to Scyld Scefing, a legendary Danish king and another floating foundling. He arrived in life in a boat no bigger than a shield. He departs in a great ship, loaded with treasure. Some of the ship-dead lie beneath the waves. Some lie beneath the earth. Some, like the Anglo-Saxon burial at Sutton Hoo, we have seen with our own eyes.

The *immrama* are Irish tales of men or monks who embark on fantastical journeys into the west. The most famous such voyage was that of Brendan the Navigator, whose story can be found in more than 120 manuscripts, written throughout the Middle Ages, in prose and poetry, in a dozen different languages. Brendan was a real person. He was a saint, one of the Twelve Apostles of Ireland. He was born in the fifth century and died in the sixth. But for a long time, everyone assumed (and, to be fair, lots of people still do assume) that the thing he is most famous for, *The Voyage of Saint Brendan the Abbot*, didn't happen. Everyone thought it was a beautiful Christian allegory. Island-hopping across the Atlantic in a tiny boat, a millennium and a half ago? Encounters with devils and weird crystal towers? Landing on a whale which turns out to be a monster?* Of *course*, it was story. Or was it?

In the late seventies, a man called Tim Severin set out to prove it might be a real account of a real voyage. His wife, a medieval literature specialist, pointed out that the *Navigatio* is different from other *immrama*: shorter on miracles, longer on practical details. Might it be possible to read the Island of Sheep, where a kind man gave Brendan hearth-cakes, and the Island of Smiths, where the sea boiled and a great stench hung in the air, as real places, as the FAROES and SOUTHEAST ICELAND – stepping stones on a northerly route to America? And so Severin decided to build a replica of an early medieval currach. Using traditional tools, the 36-foot *Brendan* was crafted out of an ash frame, lashed with leather thongs, covered with 49 ox-hides and waterproofed with wool grease. To put to sea in such a boat was, frankly, to dice with death. One Kerryman watching Severin and his four crew-mates prepare to embark remarked: 'Sure they'll make it – but they'll need a miracle.' In their first week at sea, clawing off the same shores which had wrecked the Armada, they were hit by a force 9 gale. Soaking wet, seasick, spinning

* Is this the original trope-maker? Cf. the monster-they-thought-was-a-cave in *The Empire Strikes Back* and the monster-they-thought-was-an-island in Jonny Duddle's bedtime favourite *The Pirate Cruncher.*

helplessly on wave crests, they were terrified the *Brendan* was going to disintegrate beneath them. But the boat survived that night, and all the nights to come, and made it to Newfoundland.

When Brendan saw (if he really did see) volcanoes and icebergs and pack-ice for the first time, it's no wonder his account reads as fantasy. Imagine seeing an iceberg if you'd never *heard* of icebergs. To him, it *was* fantastical, outside his experience, outside the experience of anyone he knew. Once upon a time, to wander, to travel, was to wonder whether you were dreaming. It's so different for us. I type *rockall*; ROCKALL leaps into my hand. I summon a whale; it breaches, thrashes its tail. A day's walk from the sea, I can make storm-waves roar in my ears. So perhaps we shouldn't doubt those long-ago travellers. We shouldn't question their tales. Instead, we should applaud them. Barry Lopez in *Arctic Dreams*, his classic travelogue of the north, reminds us how different Brendan and his companions were to the Viking settlers and Elizabethan colonists who followed them to the New World. 'The themes are of compassion, wonder, and respect,' he writes. 'These impeccable, generous, innocent, attentive men were, one must think, the perfect travellers.'

If you hadn't met St Brendan before, it's still likely you've read or watched a twentieth-century riff on the *immram*: C.

S. Lewis's *The Voyage of the Dawn Treader*, in which King
Caspian, three this-world children and a talking otherworld mouse sail across the sea and find Aslan at the ends
of their earth. There's a picture in my old Puffin edition
which used to terrify me: a big black cloud about to engulf
a tiny ship. Brendan, on his adventures, met something
equally mysterious, a *caligo*, which is normally translated
as *fog* – but you could choose another word, the word
Lewis uses for what's looming in front of the ship: 'It was
a Darkness.' At first the Narnians think it's land, a moun-
tain rising on their port bow, but they soon realise their
mistake: 'For a few feet in front of their bows they could
see the swell of the bright greenish-blue water. Beyond
that, they could see the water looking pale and grey as it
would look late in the evening. But beyond that again, utter
blackness as if they had come to the edge of moonless and
starless night.' They edge forwards, until they realise this
is the place where dreams come true. Dreams, how lovely,
think the children. No, say the Narnians. Not those sorts
of dreams. Not *day*dreams. Real dreams. Nightmares.

When I crossed the Doldrums, I thought of that
picture a lot. The days were hot and heavy and grey. The
sea gulped and lurched and spat. We longed for wind, for
air. And then we'd glimpse Darkness on the horizon, a
dense squall, prowling, stalking. There was no wind to sail

away. We were miles and miles from land, guarding our diesel like a dragon guards its gold. There was nothing we could do but wait for Darkness to swallow us whole. The world vanished. The wind blew from all directions and none. A gale shrieked in the shrouds. We tore off the sails, but the gale was gone. The sea was calm. All around was night-in-day and pounding rain. And then it let us go. It spat us out and moved off and away, grumbling and flickering as it went. If our copy of *World Cruising Routes* hadn't assured us that such squalls were a humdrum feature of the inter-tropical convergence zone, I'd have sworn blind we'd been visited by devils.

‡

When it came to creatures of the sea, we long argued the toss as to where lay the line between this world and the otherworld, not quite sure what belonged in port-town tavern-tales, and what belonged on the dissecting table. Now we're more confident: krakens, mermaids, unicorns, *tales*; giant squid,* narwhals, platypuses, *table*. But you sense that original uncertainty when you consider some of the names

---

* Giant and colossal squid are only just emerging from myth. When the Natural History Museum finally got hold of an almost complete 'wet' specimen in 2004, they had to ask Damien Hirst's shark-tank guys for help displaying it.

we chose. We call whales, dolphins and porpoises *cetaceans*; Cetus was the sea-monster that Perseus killed. Lugubrious manatees and pensive dugongs, we call *sirenia*, a nod to Odysseus's old adversaries, the Sirens – perhaps a more surprising choice. It's easy to think a humpback whale monstrous; harder to imagine a sea-cow's squeak so over-whelming you'd drown for her.

What's more, as recently as the end of the eighteenth century, you could still find an entry for MERMAID plum proud between MERLUCCIUS and MEROPS in a perfectly serious dictionary of natural history. William Frederic Martyn, its author, admits that some naturalists 'diſpute the exiſtence of this creature', while 'others as ſtrenuouſly affirm it'. Warning us against both credulity and undue scepticism, he concludes that 'there ſeems to be ſuffcient evidence to eſtabliſh its reality'. After all, in his day people would still pay good money for sight of a mermaid, only to find themselves squinting at the corpse of a monkey, hemmed with a fishy tail, prettied up with ribbons and silk. Did they struggle to marry the low lights, the impresario hurrying them along, the reek of decay with tales of beautiful ladies lounging on rocks?

I admit I'd never bought those stories of sailors mistak-ing seals for mermaids. Seals on rocks look like seals on rocks. You might, at a pinch, mistake a seal in the water for a doe-eyed Labrador, but for a mermaid? Never. And then I watched a silent film of *Peter Pan* (another cultural artefact dating back to 1924), and I realised I was wrong. The dozens of young women, now long-dead, slithering into the shallows in shimmery scale-suits looked *exactly* like galumphing walruses. You would, however, struggle to mistake a Disney incarnation for a pinniped. When Wendy meets the mermaids in 1953, they are Mean Girls with flicky hair, Southern-Belle accents, shell-bikinis and pouts for Peter. Recently, though, the Neverland mermaids have grown fishier, witchier, with webbed fingers and blank soulless eyes. They flash and fizz and fight like conger eels. They click and whistle like eldritch dolphins.

In the 1970s, with the publication of Elaine Morgan's *The Descent of Woman*, a bold new evolutionary idea grew legs. Mermaids, we could all agree, didn't exist.* But perhaps we, as a species, perhaps we used to live half-in, half-out of the water. Why else do we walk upright? Why are we (especially we women we) relatively fatty and hairless? Look at our offspring's diving reflex (that *Nevermind* album cover). Look how babies born in water don't take their first breath until they surface. Why do men go bald but women, by and large, don't? Because, says Morgan, 'it

---

* Although the cover of a follow-up book features Botticelli's *The Birth of Venus*, who's standing in a shell, rather like a mermaid who's just got her legs.

would be a powerful advantage for a baby if its mother's hair was long enough for his fingers to twine into; and if the hair floated around her for a yard or so on the surface he wouldn't have to make so accurate a beeline in swimming toward her when he wanted a rest.'*

Science didn't fancy her aquatic ape hypothesis, partly because it quite probably isn't true, but partly because her book flew so funnily and feministly in the face of what she calls the 'Tarzan' strand of evolutionary thinking, which says we developed our distinctive *sapiens* features, bipedalism, tools, speech etc. because big man did big hunting did kill big game. The evolutionary biologist Stephen Jay Gould calls Morgan's idea farcical – but, he says, it's no more farcical than 'more famous tall tales by and for men'.

Turns out, then, that our cultural bait-ball of women + the water + the weird goes *deep*. Algernon Charles Swinburne, a decadent Victorian aesthete with glorious wild red hair, whose *Poems and Ballads* was cancelled in the 1860s for containing too much sapphism and kink and too little God, gave us the slightly nuts poem 'The Triumph of Time'. The sea, as we already know, is linked to death: 'Find me,' he begs it, 'one grave of thy thousand graves.' But it is also a 'great sweet mother', this 'green-girdled

---

* Apologies if this is triggering for all the long-haired men and women out there who are survivors of *owwww let go!* teaching children to swim.

mother-of-mine', and (borderline oedipally) 'a lover of men'. The sea got to Byron in the same way. In the same poem we met in WARNINGS, he calls himself the ocean's child, he trusts her billows, he lays his hand upon her mane – like a little hominid clinging to his mother's hair, like a big hominid trying to touch a mermaid's curls. But the sea, you can be sure, is much more than a plaything of the male gaze.

Long ago, when my children were small enough to think their mother was as mighty as the waves, one of them came home from school with a story that blew Biff, Chip and Kipper out of the water. It was a story about a selkie, those beings, male or more often female, who can shift their shape between human and seal. We curled up and read how once upon a time a selkie was dancing on the shores of an island in HEBRIDES. We read how a fisherman took her sealskin. She stayed on land. She kept his house. She had his children. She was a good wife, a loving mother. And then ... one day ... there ... in an old trunk ... she found it. Her sealskin. She was free to go. And go she did.

A few years later, I remember showing my children some of the clothes I'd worn in my twenties, clothes I'd kept in the attic in air-locked bags. A winsome white dress spangled with red anchors. A cropped naval-punk frock-coat. Look, look, I was saying, this was Mummy once. But, of course, I'm not a selkie. I can't climb into my old skins and slip back into the sea. And yet, it occurs to me, a friend of mine has just been prescribed cold-water swimming to buck the perimenopause. The GP might as well have handed her a chit inked *be more selkie*.

The sea is death. The sea is birth. J. G. Ballard's 1962 novel, *The Drowned World*, a 'neuronic odyssey' masquerading as an adventure story, reminds us that the warm and salty seas of deep time once cradled all life on Earth. He imagines a future world of extreme heat and high seas, with the remnants of humanity huddled around the poles. London is underwater, a Triassic dreamscape of caimans, giant mosquitoes and drifting clumps of Sargasso weed. Below the water the streets and shops are intact: 'a reflection in a lake that has somehow lost its original'. From the upper floors of the Ritz, a dissolute island of silk shirts and vintage whisky, the scientist-hero records the regression of the capital's flora and fauna. Evolution is unspooling, and Dr Robert Kerans is a haggard hermit at the end of time.

He's beset by strange dreams, by hallucinations of swamps and lagoons, which take him further back in 'archaeopsychic time' than our day-before-yesterday flood myths. Do we, he wonders, carry memories of all the past ages of Earth in our spinal column? Or perhaps, he thinks, 'these sunken lagoons simply remind me of the drowned world of my uterine childhood'. The uterus is full of amniotic fluid, the sea from which we all emerge, the sea to which we can never return.* But Kerans is convinced that return he can – somewhere, somehow. He sets off in a gimcrack catamaran and crosses a vestigial Channel under towers of black cumulus, abandoning his boat in dunes of silt, walking towards the sun, in the blistering heat, towards his death, towards his blessed land.

The only time I have come close to death (except, so the story goes, at my birth), was when that breaking Pacific wave closed over my head. I wasn't underwater very long, but long enough to be quickened for months afterwards by the bright blue burst of light and life when the boat righted itself, a rebirth, if you will, the baptism I never had. Both times, the tide in the Bristol Channel, my aboriginal waters, must have been in full flood. Why? Because the lock-gates to death's harbour only open on the ebb.

The great Victorian folklorist James Frazer says this belief – this knowledge – exists up and down the Atlantic seaboard. The ebb, he says, isn't just 'a melancholy emblem of failure, of weakness, and of death'. No, for us,

---

* An *amnion* was the bowl a Homeric hero would have used to catch the blood of a religious sacrifice, an etymology so metaphorically wild, I'm reeling as if somebody had actually slaughtered a goat in front of me.

its power is real. 'People can't die, along the coast,' says David Copperfield's friend, Mr Peggotty, 'except when the tide's pretty nigh out.' John Falstaff, too, the larger-than-life companion of wild Prince Hal, before he became good King Henry, dies off-stage, 'ev'n at the turning o' th' tide'. And in 'Crossing the Bar', Tennyson imagines himself drifting out to sea, out to death, on the ebb: 'Sunset and evening star, / And one clear call for me! / And may there be no moaning of the bar, / When I put out to sea'.

Tennyson wrote the poem in 1889, three years before his death. It came to him, he said, in a flash, while making the short crossing from Lymington to Yarmouth in WIGHT. In a lovely piece of literary detective work, John Spedding points out Lymington has no bar and Yarmouth's sandbank is mute, and instead steers us west to Salcombe in PLYMOUTH, where there is a bar, which does indeed moan. Tennyson had been sailing there a few months earlier, in ill-health, in maudlin spirits, telling a friend: 'This world would mean nothing to me if there were no hereafter.' The poem was set to music for his funeral, and people who love the sea will have heard it spoken over their coffins ever since. It's not a big poem, or a clever one, but it perfectly and forever captures our dream of peace at the sunset of our lives, our dream of beauty at the ebb of our breath.

Tennyson lies in Westminster Abbey, memorialised alongside many others we've met in these chapters: Lord Byron and George Eliot, Elizabeth I and William of Orange, Charles Darwin and William Wilberforce. If you're not expecting a place amongst them, why not consider being buried at sea? There are a few dedicated spots where your body entire can be lowered into the deep, in HEBRIDES and TYNEmouth, in DOVER and WIGHT.* Sadly, it's no longer eco-friendly to be sewn into sailcloth. Perhaps a *Shipping Forecast* blanket would do the trick? (I've book-marked the link, just in case.) You then need to go inside a coffin. (I've emailed to ask whether a golden boat-shaped one is OK.) You need to weight your coffin with 200 kilo-grams – Drake's lead version would no longer pass muster – and hole it with 50 holes. Into the sea you go. And there, hopefully a bit deeper than full fathom five, you can await your slow sea-change, into coral and pearl, into something rich and strange.

---

* You do need a licence. Ashes, on the other hand, are a free swim.

POETRY

*A poet is a nightingale, who sits in darkness
and sings to cheer its own solitude with sweet
sounds; his auditors are as men entranced
by the melody of an unseen musician, who
feel that they are moved and softened,
yet know not whence or why.*

Percy Bysshe Shelley, 'A Defence of Poetry' (1821)

P ERCY BYSSHE SHELLEY WROTE AN ODE to the West
Wind, asking him to be his trumpet of prophecy, to
spread his words of freedom like 'ashes and sparks' to the
whole of mankind. Didn't he know who he was talking to?
The West Wind is an absolute monarch, not a *sans-culottes*
waving the tricolor on the barricades. No surprise then
that Shelley, as legend has it, died when he wouldn't reef
down during a Mediterranean storm, his high-spec schoo-
ner – named *Ariel* for the sprite who helped Prospero raise
that tempest – sinking under full sail.

Without this propensity to live fast and die young, more
of the Romantic poets might have lived long enough to
read Robert FitzRoy's first meteorological notices in the
Times. They mightn't have thought much of the man: a
stuffed shirt, too straight-edge. They mightn't have thought
much of the forecasts, either. There goes science, with its
cold touch, clipping the wings of the angels, emptying the

haunted air, unweaving rainbows (John Keats, dead at 25). All knowledge comes to grief; the Tree of Knowledge isn't the Tree of *Life* (Byron, dead at 36). But what this chapter is really about is how Shelley (dead at 29), for all his radical politics, would have struggled to conceive of such a revolution in poetics that an admiral's prosy predictions could one day resonate like an Aeolian harp, that a maritime forecast could acquire the numinosity, the prestige, the very name of poetry. How, then, did our idea of poetry change so much that –

> *I turn from you, and listen to the wind,*
> *Which long has raved unnoticed*

and

Northeasterly 7 to severe gale 9, occasionally storm 10 at first

– both count?

At the high tide of the Romantic movement, some sharp-eyed observers, high up in the critical crow's-nest, already saw the coming storm. In his essay 'The Four Ages of Poetry', the satirist Thomas Love Peacock took aim against 'the rant of unregulated passion, the whining of exaggerated feeling, and the cant of factitious sentiment'. It was frankly childish, he said, for grown men to 'cry to be charmed to sleep by the jingle of silver bells'. But through-out the Victorian era, those bells didn't so much jingle and jangle, as toll munificently.

At the beginning of the twentieth century, however, the intellectual elite grew annoyed that not only the bourgeoisie, but even *women* and *the working classes* were starting, thanks to the broadening of education and the rise of English as proper academic subject, to appreciate Shelley, Keats, Byron and co. It was vital, therefore, if the elite were to remain elite, to come up with a way to make poetry unappealing and inaccessible, to make it easier to look down on saps who liked nice poems about autumn, tossing daffodils etc.

One result (a cog in the mighty machine of modern-ism) was Imagist poetry. Explained Terry Eagleton in his hugely popular *Literary Theory: An Introduction,* 'Language had gone soft and lost its virility: it needed to be stiffened up again, made hard and stone-like, reconnected with the physical world. The ideal Imagist poem would be a laconic three-line affair of gritty images, like an army officer's rapped-out command.'

Or like …

THE *SHIPPING FORECAST*!!!

Out out thou deep and dark blue ocean. In in you chrome and stylish lido. Adieu Aeolus. Hola Met Office.

I'm imagining the young man who wrote the first proto-*Shipping Forecast* for 1 January 1924 as a poet manqué. He's the same age as the century, too young to have fought in the Great War, old enough to feel bad that he didn't. He is clever, sensitive, but he was forced to abandon his dreams of English and university by an insensitive petit-bourgeois father. On New Year's Eve 1923, then, he is finishing up work as a clerk in the Meteorological Office, nested inside the Air Ministry at Holborn. His department head limps over to his desk. Says he's got a job for him. Tomorrow morning. This new bulletin thingy. You're a smart chap. You write it up for us. Short and sweet. Righto? Righto. After work, our clerk (in my head, he's called Leonard) walks a few streets north to spend an hour in the British Museum's Round Reading Room before it closes.

Keen to get his head round the new ideas in poetry, he's reserved Ezra Pound's 'A Few Don'ts by an Imagiste' and a collection of up-to-the-minute verse with an introduction by the American poet Amy Lowell. Pound, he finds intimidating. But Lowell is lucid and encouraging. More than encouraging. Hurriedly, he copies out her advice, retrieves his coat, hat and umbrella, and rushes out onto the streets of Bloomsbury. He's so excited, he hardly knows what to do with himself. He wanders in a daze, losing his way in the fog, arriving home to find his landlady tetchy and his liver and onions cold. But what does he care?

If he clings to Amy Lowell's guidelines – tight, he thinks, as a shipwrecked sailor to a storm-tossed rock, before remembering he's meant to dismiss that sort of simile as Victorian pap – he will, he's sure of it, create a work for the ages. Those sneering men in the Reading Room, who wince at his scuffed boots, his grubby collar, his Stoke Newington accent, what will become of *their* work? Nothing! Their paltry efforts will be strewn along the tideline, picked over, if they're lucky, by the odd doctoral student. His poem – his 'Weather Shipping'* – will live forever. He unfolds his scribbled notes, those guidelines –

1. Use common speech
2. Create new rhythms: a new cadence = a new idea
3. Absolute freedom in the choice of subject
4. Particulars NOT vague generalities (however magnificent and sonorous!!)
5. Be hard and clear, *never* blurred nor indefinite
6. ~~Concentration~~ distillation is very essence of poetry

---

* The title change came later.

– gets to work, and lo! the *Shipping Forecast* as 'Shipping Forecast' was born.

We don't know what happened to him afterwards. Did a kind boss, who'd lost his sons in the war, take him under his wing? Did he marry well, have four children, who rolled their eyes whenever 'Daddy's' forecast came on the radiogram? Or did he take up communism, meet a beautiful young man, and go to fight and die in the Spanish Civil War? We don't know – and we don't need to know. Why? Because its lack of author places 'Shipping Forecast' hand in glove with mid-century poetics.

From the relatively safe harbour of New Criticism, through the intricate lock-gates of structuralism, and out onto the savage post-structuralist sea, the author becomes increasingly redundant: a supernumerary on the poem's voyage. So if, for example, a Radio 4 insider were to apparate right now and say, 'Hang on just on a minute! You haven't a clue! The *Shipping Forecast* isn't a *poem*. It's a *weather* bulletin. You and your cheek—' we absolutely and categorically do not have to listen. We can politely tell them not to fall for what the New Critics, who ruled the roost in the 1930s–50s, called the 'intentional fallacy', which states, baldly, that the author's intentions matter not one jot. The poem's the thing. We don't care what its author meant.

The Frenchman Roland Barthes, one of the biggest beasts of the post-war literary theory firmament, whose acolytes otherwise found the pernickety fossicking of New Criticism *pas trop cool*, backed them to the hilt on this point. In his essay, 'The Death of the Author', he reminds us that primitive people understood this truth: the *I* who tells a story is not important; the shaman is merely a conduit; Homer was many homers.* But today (1967, if you'll forgive the chronologic context), the 'image of literature to be found in contemporary culture is tyrannically centred on the author, his person, his history, his tastes, his passions'. Time to careen the poem, to haul it out of the water, to prop it high and dry, and scrub its hull furiously, ridding it of biographical barnacles, of socio-economic seaweed, until it is sleek, shiny and seaworthy once more.

Nor was 'Shipping Forecast' missing in action during the wave of counterculture protests that swept the world a year later. Ask any standard-issue *soixante-huitard* what they thought of the Met Office, and they'd have told you *bof*, to be sure with its powerful all-seeing eye, this organ of the state is an example *classique* of Monsieur Foucault's

---

* Thus when different people read 'Shipping Forecast', we admire them in the same way that archaic Greeks admired their rhapsodes: we praise their voice, their performance, their mastery of the form, not their personal creativity.

celebrated panopticon, is it not?* And this *Sheeping Forecast*, with its strait-laced semiotic systems, its dull, discrete packages of signs, is it not a supreme artefact of bourgeois oppression? Again, we'd have to say *non*. 'Shipping Forecast' has revolution baked in. Superficially, it appears so authoritative, so declarative: there will be *this* weather *here*, there will be *that* weather *there*. And yet, any future-tense statement about the weather contains an implicit possibility that the statement will prove false. Each forecast area, each verse, offers a claim to truth and an immediate counter-claim, meaning 'Shipping Forecast' explicitly resists its own authority, earning its place on the barricades.

As a poem, 'Shipping Forecast' also anticipated the moment when the spotlight of critical attention, which had already turned away from the author, swivelled to illuminate the reader. The buttoned-up New Critics had thought it was bad form to care about our individual reactions to a poem. They even had a matchy-matchy name for it: the affective fallacy. This would have been problematic for 'Shipping Forecast', which was increasingly dancing an affecting *pas de deux* with each of its reader-listeners. Thankfully, towards the end of twentieth century,

---

* Timeline blur alert no. 2.

we started to acknowledge that the reader-listener is not a monolith; s/he is legion.

Just as we shouldn't assume that every reader of Albert Camus is a cliff-faced French dude with a Gitanes stuck to his lip, so we shouldn't assume that everyone brings an iden-tikit listening game to 'Shipping Forecast'. For some, even for many, the poem will have positive associations: warmth tea home nostalgia chips childhood joy breakers adven-ture. But what about the woman who remembers how as a little girl she was meant to finish her tea by six o'clock so she could go upstairs for her bath, how her mother (who can't find her bloody sealskin) would be angry if she didn't finish; for her, FISHER, GERMAN BIGHT isn't magi-cal or mystical, isn't patriotic or adventurous, but lumps of love and gristle that are refusing to go down. Or what about John Prescott, former ship's steward, Hull MP and Labour deputy prime minister, who was invited to read 'Shipping Forecast' for Comic Relief in 2011. When he landed on his home waters, he growled UMBER, breaking off to remind us that's how 'we say it up there', an on-the-spot piece of reception theory analysis about how it feels to hear disembodied RP voices misspeak your name. How, we must then ask ourselves, would 'Shipping Forecast' sound to a young Iranian boy whose father drowned when his family crossed at DOVER?

After pointing to the reader, the compass swung to the author again – *not* to the original author, but an entirely new entity instead: the reader-as-author. As Terry Eagleton explains: 'The reader or critic shifts from the role of the consumer to that of producer.' In recent decades, like hip-hop artists sampling drum-breaks, creatives of all stripes have started to chop up 'Shipping Forecast', to transpose it to different media, to different genres, creating new rafts of meaning, like reader-mutineers on the *Bounty* setting the author-Bligh adrift.*

When I begged my 14-year-old daughter to ask her WhatsApp groups what they knew about the *Shipping Forecast*, at first there was no sound but an appalled crackle of static … and then one girl piped up: 'Blur wrote a song about it.' YESSS! GOLD STAR! Blur's third album, *Parklife*, released in 1994, is an affectionate, funny, rueful, mocking, sharp, elegiacal tour of Britain. It closes with 'This Is a Low' – quick, if you don't already know it, listen now! – rightly hailed as one of the songs of the decade. John Harris, in *The Last Party*, his account of Britpop's Cool Britannia moment, says Damon Albarn's lyrics 'infuse

---

* The modernist poets were already on to this. If 'Shipping Forecast' had been written a little earlier, you can bet it would have featured in T. S. Eliot's *The Waste Land*, which is awash with water imagery and fragments of mass-culture both.

both the British climate and landscape with a drama as affecting as any of the myths surrounding America, tying its wonders to the subtle magic of the shipping forecast'. And what's most inspiring is how, despite what he calls Blur's fascination with 'failure, delusion and farce', we don't come away down-hearted. The reverse! Britain, Blur sort of says, isn't a history-defying superpower, but you know what? It doesn't matter. We're *alright*.

The poet Seamus Heaney, whose 'Glanmore Sonnets, VII' uses 'Shipping Forecast' to soundtrack the peace of his new 'hedge-school' home in the Irish countryside after the upsurge and flux of Troubles-era Belfast, gives us what he modestly calls 'a' view of poetry in an essay called 'Feeling into Words'. Poetry, he says, is divination; poetry is a revelation of the self to the self. Poems, he says, contain elements of continuity; we dig into poems like we dig into the past, finding the buried shard as important as the buried city. So far, so very 'Shipping Forecast'. But poetry, he says, can also restore the culture to itself. I was thinking about that, wondering how it might work, when – to my delight – I came across a recording of 'The People's Shipping Forecast'.

In it, the poet and performer Murray Lachlan Young, playing the shaman, the rhapsode, acts as the conduit for the creative spark of listeners across the land; listeners who, in their hundreds, had sent Radio 4 snippets about their lives, using the distinctive 'Shipping Forecast' syntax as their poetic form. Young spliced those snippets together to create one collective poem, which tacks confidently between cancer and buttocks, toddlers and tax returns, dissertations and Labradors, ironing and the school run: 'paint roller 1 or 2, magnolia, increasing slowly … knitting, storm force 9, baby soon … anticipation, daughter's birthday 4, cake rising very very slowly,' and, for all you Radio 4 fangirls and boys out there, 'Archers, Rob, Sinisterre, Helen, visibility rising slowly'.*

Not every day can be a high or an adventure or a revolution. Days are rarely game-changing. Or world-beating. Instead, days are mostly (thanks, Philip Larkin, high priest of the day to day) where we live. And the *Shipping Forecast*'s poetical superpower, day in day out, is to turn every day's everydayness into hallowed ground, and for that I – and many, many others – am truly thankful.

Amen.

---

* IYKYK.

GLANMORE SONNETS

by Seamus Heaney

VII.

Dogger, Rockall, Malin, Irish Sea:
Green, swift upsurges, North Atlantic flux
Conjured by that strong gale-warning voice
Collapse into a sibilant penumbra.
Midnight and closedown. Sirens of the tundra,
Of eel-road, seal-road, keel-road, whale-road, raise
Their wind-compounded keen behind the baize
And drive the trawlers to the lee of Wicklow.
L'Etoile, Le Guillemot, La Belle Hélène
Nursed their bright names this morning in the bay
That toiled like mortar. It was marvellous
And actual, I said out loud, 'A haven,'
The word deepening, clearing, like the sky
Elsewhere on Minches, Cromarty, The Faroes.

THE SHIPPING FORECAST

by John O'Donnell

for my father

Tied up at the pier in darkened harbour
the two of us below, in cabin's amber
light; me surly in a sleeping-bag, fifteen,
and you, past midnight, calmly tuning in
to the Shipping Forecast, Long Wave's
crackle, hiss, until you find the voice.
What's next for us: rain or fair? There are
warnings of gales in Rockall and Finisterre.
So near now, just this teak bulkhead
between us, and yet so apart, battened
hatches as another low approaches, the high
over Azores as distant as a man is from a boy.
I think of my own boat one day, the deep.
Beside me the sea snores, turns over in its sleep.

PRAYER

by Carol Ann Duffy

Some days, although we cannot pray, a prayer
utters itself. So, a woman will lift
her head from the sieve of her hands and stare
at the minims sung by a tree, a sudden gift.

Some nights, although we are faithless, the truth
enters our hearts, that small familiar pain;
then a man will stand stock-still, hearing his youth
in the distant Latin chanting of a train.

Pray for us now. Grade I piano scales
console the lodger looking out across
a Midlands town. Then dusk, and someone calls
a child's name as though they named their loss.

Darkness outside. Inside, the radio's prayer –
Rockall. Malin. Dogger. Finisterre.

REFERENCES

WEATHER

Conrad, Joseph. *The Mirror of the Sea* (Methuen & Co., 1935 [first published 1906]).

WARNINGS

Aristotle. *Meteorologica*, trans. H. D. P. Lee (Loeb Classical Library, 1953).

Austen, Jane. *Sanditon* (Penguin Books, 2019 [first published posthumously, 1925]).

BBC News. 'Weather forecasting's post-1987 revolution' (11 October 2017).

Brayne, Martin. *The Greatest Storm: Britain's Night of Destruction, November 1703* (The History Press, 2002).

Byron, Lord George. *Childe Harold's Pilgrimage* (Project Gutenberg, 2013 [first published 1812–18]).

Cohen, Robin. *Frontiers of Identity: The British and the Others* (Routledge, 2024 [first published 1994]).

Cowper, William. *The Works of William Cowper, Comprising His Poems, Correspondence, and Translations* (H. G. Bohn, 1854).

Defoe, Daniel. *The Storm* (Penguin Books, 2005 [first published 1704]).

FitzRoy, Robert. *The Weather Book: A Manual of Practical Meteorology* (Longman, Green, Longman, Roberts & Green, 1863).

Fowler, Frank. *The Wreck of the Royal Charter* (Sampson Low, Son & Co., 1859).

Harding, Jeremy. 'The Arrestables', *The London Review of Books* (16 April 2020).

Jones, Tamsin Treverton. *Windblown: Landscape, Legacy and Loss: The Great Storm of 1987* (Hodder & Stoughton, 2017).

Met Office. 'Lessons and Legacy of the Great Storm of 1987', https://www.metoffice.gov.uk/about-us/who -we-are/our-history/lessons-and-legacy-of-the-great-storm-of-1987 (accessed 15 August 2024).

Moore, Peter. *The Weather Experiment: The Pioneers Who Sought to See the Future* (Vintage Publishing, 2016).

New Internationalist. 'Between the devil and the deep blue sea' (27 November 2018).

New York Times. 'LATEST BY TELEGRAPH.; The Overland Pacific Mails--The Cass-Yrissari Treaty--Utah Affairs, &c. FROM WASHINGTON' (19 August 1858).

Newby, Eric. *The Last Grain Race* (Penguin Books, 1958 [first published 1956]).

Raban, Jonathan. *The Oxford Book of the Sea* (Oxford University Press, 1992).

Ruskin, John. *The Harbours of England* (George Allen, 1895).

MAPS

Ascherson, Neal. 'At the British Museum: Celts', *London Review of Books* (22 October 2015).

Brannigan, John. "'Dreaming of the Islands": The Poetry of the Shipping Forecast', *UCDScholarcast* (spring 2010).

Carolan, Victoria. 'The shipping forecast and British national identity', *Journal for Maritime Research* (13:2, 2011, pp. 104–116).

Chaucer, Geoffrey. *The Riverside Chaucer* (Oxford University Press, 2008 [first published fourteenth century]).

Conrad, Joseph. *Heart of Darkness* (Penguin Books, 2012 [first published 1899]).

Davies, Norman. *The Isles: A History* (Pan Macmillan, 1999).

Duffy, Carol Ann. *Mean Time* (Pan Macmillan 2017 [first published 1993]).

Fox, Kate. *Watching the English: The Hidden Rules of English Behaviour* (Hodder & Stoughton, 2004).

Gentleman, Amelia. *The Windrush Betrayal: Exposing the Hostile Environment* (Guardian Faber Publishing, 2019).

Harris, Alexandra. *Weatherland: Writers & Artists Under English Skies* (Thames & Hudson, 2015).

Jeffs, Amy. *Storyland: A New Mythology of Britain* (Quercus, 2021).

Light, Alison. 'YOUNG BESS: Historical novels and growing up', *Feminist Review* (33:1, 1989, pp. 57–71).

Mabey, Richard. *Turned Out Nice Again: On Living with the Weather* (Profile Books, 2013).

O'Farrell, John. 'How to Pass for British', *Guardian* (9 February 2002).

Pye, Michael. *The Edge of the World: How the North Sea Made Us What We Are* (Penguin Books, 2014).

CROSSINGS

Caesar, Julius. *The Gallic War*, trans. Cynthia Damon (Loeb Classical Library, 2016).

Conrad, Joseph. *Heart of Darkness* (Penguin Books, 2012 [first published 1899]).

Economist. 'Why Small Boats Are a Big Problem for Britain' (2 November 2022).

Hogben, Lawrence. 'The Most Important Weather Forecast in History', *London Review of Books* (26 May 1994).

International Organization for Migration. 'Missing Migraints Project', https://missingmigrants.iom.int (accessed 15 August 2024).

Jesse, John Heneage. *Memoirs of the Court of England During the Reign of the Stuarts* (George Bell and Son, 1889 [first published 1840]).

London Gazette. 'OPERATION "DYNAMO" – NARRATIVE OF EVENTS' (15 July 1947).

Longmate, Norman. *Defending the Island: From Caesar to the Armada* (Pimlico, 2001 [first published 1991])

Longmate, Norman. *Island Fortress: The Defence of Great Britain 1603–1945* (Pimlico, 2001 [first published 1991]).

Marshall, H. E. *Our Island Story* (Thomas Nelson and Sons, 1952 [first published 1905]).

Mattingly, Garrett. *The Armada* (The Riverside Press, 1959).

Met Office. 'D-Day – The Most Important Weather Forecast in History', https://www.metoffice.gov.uk/about-us/who-we-are/our-history/met-office-d-dayweather-forecast (accessed 15 August 2024).

Nancollas, Tom. *The Ship Asunder: A Maritime History of Britain in Eleven Vessels* (Penguin Books, 2022).

Nelson, Lord Horatio. *The Dispatches and Letters of Vice Admiral Lord Viscount Nelson* (Henry Colburn, 1845).

Stevenson, Robert Louis. 'The English Admirals', *Virginibus Puerisque* (Penguin Books, 1946 [first published 1881]).

Taylor, Michael. *The Interest: How the British Establishment Resisted the Abolition of Slavery* (Vintage Publishing, 2021).

Uglow, Jenny. *In These Times: Living in Britain through Napoleon's Wars, 1793–1815* (Faber & Faber, 2014).

William of Poitiers. 'The Deeds of William, Duke of the Normans and King of the English', *English Historical Documents: 1042–1189* (Routledge, 1996).

Williams, Eric. *British Historians and the West Indies* (Africana Publishing Corporation, 1972 [first published 1964]).

Wordsworth, William. 'To the Men of Kent', *The Collected Poems of William Wordsworth* (Read Books, 2020 [poem first published 1803]).

TIDELINE

Anonymous. *The Epic of Gilgamesh: The Babylonian Epic Poem and Other Texts in Akkadian and Sumerian*, trans. Andrew George (Penguin Books, 2002).

Baxter, Stephen. *Flood* (Orion Publishing, 2009).

Conway, Ed. *Material World: A Substantial Story of Our Past and Future* (Ebury Publishing, 2023).

Grieve, Hilda. *The Great Tide: The Story of the 1953 Flood Disaster in Essex* (County Council of Essex, 1959).

Defoe, Daniel. *The Collected Works of Daniel Defoe* (Digicat, 2022 [essay first published 1722]).

Johnson, Ben. *The Devil Is an Ass* (Project Gutenberg, 2015 [first published 1631]).

Lanchester, John. *The Wall* (Faber & Faber, 2019).

Meek, James. 'Underwater Living', *London Review of Books* (5 January 2023).

Met Office. 'UK sea level projections to 2030', https://www.metoffice.gov.uk/research/news/2019/uk-sea-level-projections-to-2300 (accessed 15 August 2024).

Nunn, Patrick D. and Compatangelo-Soussignan, Rita. 'The drowning of "Lyonesse": early legends of land submergence in southwest Britain and geoscience', (*Folk Life: Journal of Ethnological Studies* (62:1, 2024, pp. 1–17).

Petridis, Alexis. 'How an ex-Vegas dancer made the first Cornish-language psych-pop album', *Guardian* (13 March 2018).

Pliny. *Natural History* (Penguin Classics, 1991).

Pye, Michael. *The Edge of the World: How the North Sea Made Us What We Are* (Penguin Books, 2014).

Rees, Gareth E. *Sunken Lands* (Elliott & Thompson, 2024).

Sebald, W. G. *The Rings of Saturn* (Vintage Publishing, 2020 [first published 1995]).

Shelley, Percy. 'Ozymandias', *Selected Poems and Prose* (Penguin Books, 2017 [poem first published 1818]).

Tennyson, Lord Alfred. *Idylls of the King* (Penguin Books, 1989 [poems first published between 1859 and 1885]).

Warner, Marina. 'The Flood', *London Review of Books* (6 March 2014).

Woolf, Virginia. *To the Lighthouse* (Penguin Books, 2018 [first published 1927]).

BOOTY

Alvarez, Al. *Offshore: A North Sea Journey* (Sceptre, 1987).

Chan, Szu Ping and Leake, Jonathan. 'Why the death of North Sea oil is a disaster for Britain', *Telegraph* (7 April 2024).

Economist. 'How Britain's dirtiest region hopes to become a hub for clean energy' (26 March 2024).

Faludi, Susan. *Stiffed: The Roots of Modern Male Rage* (William Morrow & Company, 2019 [first published 1999]).

Gillett, Edward. *A History of Grimsby* (OUP, 1970).

Goddard, John and Spalding, Roger. *Fish 'n' Ships: The Rise and Fall of Grimsby* (Dalesman Publishing, 1987).

Harvie, Christopher. *Fool's Gold: The Story of North Sea Oil* (Hamish Hamilton, 1994).

Jack, Ian. *Before the Oil Ran Out: Britain, 1978–86* (Vintage Publishing, 1996).

Lasley, Tabitha. *Sea State* (Fourth Estate, 2022).

Meek, James. 'Why are you still here?', *London Review of Books* (23 April 2015).

Melville, Herman. *Redburn* (Penguin Books, 1976 [first published 1849]).

Murray, Donald S. *Herring Tales: How the Silver Darlings Shaped Human Taste and History* (Bloomsbury Natural History, 2015)

Naughtie, James. 'Oil: A Crude History of Britain' (BBC Sounds, 2015).

Raban, Jonathan. *Coasting* (Picador, 1995).

Reilly, M. S. J. 'Mortality from Occupational Accidents to

United Kingdom Fishermen 1961–80', *British Journal of Industrial Medicine* (42: 12, Dec. 1985), pp. 806–14.

Shepherd, Mike. *Oil Strike North Sea: A First-Hand History of North Sea Oil* (Luath Press, 2015).

Woolf, Virginia. *To the Lighthouse* (Penguin Books, 2018 [first published 1927]).

SOLO

Ballantyne, R. M. *The Coral Island* (Penguin Random House Children's, 1994 [first published 1857]).

Bates, Michael. *Holding the Fort* (Principality of Sealand, 2015).

Colley, Linda. *Captives: Britain, Empire and the World 1600–1850* (Vintage Publishing, 2003).

Defoe, Daniel. *The Life and Adventures of Robinson Crusoe* (Project Gutenberg, 1996 [first published 1719]).

Donne, John. 'Meditation XVII', *The Complete English Poems* (Penguin Classics, 1976 [poem first published 1624]).

Donoghue, Emma. *Haven* (Pan Macmillan, 2023).

Golding, William. *The Lord of the Flies* (Faber & Faber, 1997 [first published 1954]).

Graeber, David. *Pirate Enlightenment, or the Real Libertalia* (Penguin Books, 2023).

'Gruinard Island X-Base Anthrax Trials 1942–43', [YouTube video] https://www.youtube.com/watch?v=6Mykjxkwwe0 (accessed 15 August 2024).

Jamie, Kathleen. 'A Lone Enraptured Male', *London Review of Books* (6 March 2008).

Johnson, Captain Charles. *A General History of the Pyrates* (Project Gutenberg, 2012 [first published 1724]).

Matar, Nabil I. *Islam in Britain, 1558–1685* (Cambridge University Press, 1998).

Nicolson, Adam. *Sea Room: An Island Life* (HarperCollins, 2002).

Norway, Arthur H. *Highways and Byways in Devon and Cornwall* (Macmillan, 1898).

Schalansky, Judith. *Atlas of Remote Islands: Fifty Islands I Have Not Visited and Never Will* (Penguin Books, 2010).

Sealand [website]. 'History of a Nation', https://sealandgov.org/pages/the-story (accessed August 15 2024).

Shakespeare, William. *The Tempest* (Penguin Classics, 2015 [first performed 1611]).

Shipway, George. *Imperial Governor* (Orion Publishing, 2002 [first published 1968]).

Tacitus. *Agricola. Germania. Dialogue on Oratory*, trans. M. Hutton and W. Peterson (Loeb Classical Libraary, 1989).

White, T. H. *The Master: An Adventure Story* (Jonathan Cape, 1957).

STORY

Chichester, Francis. *Gipsy Moth Circles the World* (Hodder and Stoughton, 1967).

Eliot, George. *Daniel Deronda*. (Penguin Books, 1995 [first published 1876]).

Knox-Johnston, Robin. *A World of My Own: The First Ever Non-Stop Solo Round the World Voyage* (Adlard Coles, 2004 [first published 1969]).

MacArthur, Ellen. 'The surprising thing I learned sailing solo around the world', https://www.youtube.com/watch?v=ooIxHVXgLbc (March 2015).

MacArthur, Ellen. *Taking on the World* (Michael Joseph, 2002).

Marsh, James, director. *The Mercy* (Studio Canal, 2017).

Moitessier, Bernard. *The Long Way*, trans. William Rodarmor (Sheridan House, 1995).

Nichols, Peter. *A Voyage for Madmen* (Profile Books, 2011 [first published 2001]).

O'Donnell, Barry. 'The Fastnet Race 1979', *British Medical Journal* (281: Dec. 1980, pp. 20–7).

Rousmaniere, John. *Fastnet Force 10: The Deadliest Storm in the History of Modern Sailing* (W. W. Norton & Co., 1993).

Royal Yachting Association and Royal Ocean Racing Club. '1979 Fastnet Race Inquiry', https://archive.org/details/fastnet-race-inquiry (accessed 15 August 2024).

Telegraph. 'The Seagirl' (6 February 2005).

Tomalin, Nicholas and Hall, Ron. *The Strange Last Voyage of Donald Crowhurst* (Hodder & Stoughton, 2016 [first published 1970]).

OTHERWORLD

Anonymous. *The Voyage of Saint Brendan: Journey to the Promised Land*, trans. John Joseph O'Meara (Dolmen Press, 1978).

Ballard, J. G. *The Drowned World* (HarperCollins, 2006 [first published 1962]).

Dickens, Charles. *David Copperfield* (Penguin Books, 2012 [first published 1850]).

Frazer, James. *The Golden Bough: A Study of Magic and Religion* (Macmillan, 1957 [first published 1890]).

Gould, Stephen Jay. *The Mismeasure of Man* (W. W. Norton & Co., 1996)

Lewis, C. S. *The Voyage of the Dawn Treader* (Puffin Books, 1973 [first published 1952]).

Lopez, Barry. *Arctic Dreams* (Picador, 1987 [first published 1986]).

Melville, Herman. *Moby Dick* (Penguin Books, 2012 [first published 1851]).

Morgan, Elaine. *The Descent of Woman: The Classic Study of Evolution* (Souvenir Press, 2006 [first published 1972]).

Sebald, W. G. *The Rings of Saturn* (Vintage Publishing, 2020 [first published 1995]).

Severin, Tim. *The Brendan Voyage* (Hutchinson, 1978).

Shakespeare, William. *Henry V* (Oxford University Press, 2008 [written *c*.1599]).

Spedding, John. 'CROSSING THE BAR: WHAT BAR?' *Tennyson Research Bulletin* (10:2, 2013, pp. 175–80).

Swinburne, Algernon Charles. 'The Triumph of Time', *Poems and Ballads* (Penguin Classics, 2000 [first published 1866]).

Tennyson, Lord Alfred. 'Crossing the Bar', *Selected Poems: Tennyson* (Penguin Classics, 2007 [poem first published 1889]).

POETRY

Barthes, Roland. 'The Death of the Author', *Image Music Text* (HarperCollins, 1993 [essay first published 1967]).

Coleridge, Samuel Taylor. 'Dejection: An Ode', *The Complete Poems of Samuel Taylor Coleridge* (Penguin Classics, 1997 [poem first published 1802]).

Eagleton, Terry. *Literary Theory: An Introduction* (Blackwell, 1983).

Harris, John. *The Last Party: Britpop, Blair and the Demise of English Rock* (Harper Collins, 2004).

Heaney, Seamus. 'Feeling into Words', *Preoccupations: Selected Prose 1968–78* (Faber & Faber, 1980).

Heaney, Seamus. 'Glanmore Sonnets, VII', *New Selected Poems, 1966–1987* (Faber & Faber, 2002).

Lowell, Amy. 'On Imagism', *Tendencies in Modern American Poetry* (New York: Macmillan Company, 1917).

Peacock, Thomas Love. 'The Four Ages of Poetry', *The Works of Thomas Love Peacock* (Legare Street Press, 2022 [essay first published 1820]).

Pound, Ezra. 'A Few Don'ts by an Imagiste', Poetry Foundation, https://www.poetryfoundation.org/poetrymagazine/articles/58900/a-few-donts-by-an-imagiste (first published 1913).

Prescott, John. 'John Prescott reads the Shipping Forecast', https://www.bbc.co.uk/sounds/play/p02prwt7 (BBC Sounds, 2011).

Shelley, Percy Bysshe. 'A Defence of Poetry', *Essays, Letters from Abroad, Translations and Fragments* (Hardpress, 2019 [first published 1840]).

Met Office. 'Shipping: Fact sheet 8 – The Shipping Forecast', 2015, https://www.metoffice.gov.uk/binaries/content/assets/metofficegovuk/pdf/research/library-and-archive/library/publications/factsheets/factsheet_8-shipping-forecast.pdf (accessed 15 August 2024).

Young, Murray Lachlan. 'The People's Shipping Forecast', 2015, https://www.bbc.co.uk/programmes/articles/3zW5TLdY6q1K17bBjKmwnZG/the-peoples-shipping-forecast (accessed 15 August 2024).

ACKNOWLEDGEMENTS

First, the hugest thank you to my editor, Céline Nyssens. I was taking a very on-brand holiday in VIKING (rain then showers, if you want to know) when she got in touch to ask would I be interested in writing something about the *Shipping Forecast*. OMIGOD WHAT ARE YOU KIDDING YES!!! She's been encouraging and enthusiastic, incisive and meticulous, curious and creative – in short, an all-round joy to work with.

Gratitude, now and forevermore, to my agent, Victoria Hobbs. A firm hand on the tiller, whatever the weather.

My thanks, also, to Jess Anderson, Miranda Ward, David Campbell, Jonathan Baker and David Eldridge for taking a raggedy old Word document and turning it into something so shipshape.

I've also really appreciated Radio 4's backing from first pitch to final draft – not to mention the love they've lavished on the *Shipping Forecast* for the past 100 years.

Shout out to the staff and volunteers at Bishops Lydeard Community Library, my lifesavers.

My biggest debt, though, is to my parents. Like a pair of redoubtable bosuns, they've helped me beat this book to quarters. They've given me ideas, confidence, reading. They've checked facts. They've proofed proofs. (All remaining errors I claim for myself!) But most of all, they've buoyed me with unstinting practical support. Without them, my dog, my weeds, my belly, my children would all be in a sorry state. Plus, if you've read this far, you'll know there's not a snowball's chance in hell I'd be writing this if I hadn't bobbed up in such a sea-going family.

I'd also especially like to thank Chris, brother and shipmate, to whom this book is dedicated. Firstly, Céline would never have tapped me up to write this if we hadn't already written *Sea Fever* together, and *Sea Fever* was all his delightful idea. Secondly, without him, I'd never have had the guts to cross BISCAY all those moons ago. In fact, as soon as he disembarked for university, I rammed a harbour wall on Gran Canaria, but that's another story. Thirdly, rrrrr!

Finally, all my love and thanks to Rupert, Rowan and Bruno, best ever home crew. Our greatest watery adventure has been a holiday on a Thames canalboat, which you might think was pretty small beer – unless and until you've spent a week afloat with a giant Irish Setter

who's triggered by a) cows, b) lock-gates and c) reverse gear. You're so good to me when I'm on deadline and haunting the house like a giant unwashed albatross. Thanks for always being there for me when I come flapping back to shore.

ABOUT THE AUTHOR

Meg Clothier studied Classics at Cambridge, sailed from England to Alaska and worked as a journalist in London and Moscow. She has written three historical novels and also *Sea Fever*, a book of seaside curiosities and maritime lore, with her brother, Chris. She lives on the sunny side of the Quantock Hills with her husband, two children and an improbable number of vegetables.